FREEDOM
LIBRARIES

FREEDOM LIBRARIES

The Untold Story of Libraries for African Americans in the South

Mike Selby

ROWMAN & LITTLEFIELD
Lanham • Boulder • New York • London

Published by Rowman & Littlefield
An imprint of The Rowman & Littlefield Publishing Group, Inc.
4501 Forbes Boulevard, Suite 200, Lanham, Maryland 20706
www.rowman.com

6 Tinworth Street, London, SE11 5AL, United Kingdom

British Library Cataloguing in Publication Information Available

Library of Congress Cataloging-in-Publication Data

Names: Selby, Mike, 1967– author.
Title: Freedom libraries : the untold story of libraries for African
    Americans in the South / Mike Selby.
Description: Lanham : Rowman & Littlefield, [2019] | Includes bibliographical
    references and index.
Identifiers: LCCN 2019013884 (print) | LCCN 2019021202 (ebook) | ISBN
    9781538115541 (electronic) | ISBN 9781538115534 (cloth : alk. paper)
Subjects: LCSH: African Americans and libraries—Southern
    States—History—20th century. | Civil rights movements—Southern
    States—History—20th century. | Mississippi Freedom Project.
Classification: LCC Z711.9 (ebook) | LCC Z711.9 .S45 2019 (print) | DDC
    027.6/309750904—dc23
LC record available at https://lccn.loc.gov/2019013884

♾™ The paper used in this publication meets the minimum requirements of
American National Standard for Information Sciences—Permanence of Paper
for Printed Library Materials, ANSI/NISO Z39.48-1992.

Contents

Preface

OUR MEMORIES define us.

I was only ten when my father took me to see *Star Wars*—a moment in time that produced such a profound cluster of emotions that the memory has resonated with me ever since. My hometown had but one theater, and the line that poured out of its front entrance was so large it had wrapped its way down an entire city block. So many people had turned out that the police were forced to barricade the street from traffic. Somehow the building accommodated everyone; even the police made it in before the main feature. Being there with my father sparked simultaneous feelings of safety, warmth, and belonging. The absolute sense of wonder that night produced such an emotional weight that I knew I would never feel that way again.

But I did.

Thirty-five years later, I stood outside the University of Alabama's Foster Auditorium during my first day of library school. My feet were on sacred ground, as fifty years before me another student stood here on her first day of library school. Her name was Autherine Lucy, and—due to a variance of pigmentation in her skin—her presence ignited one of the worst race riots in the history of the state. The same scenario played out seven years later, when two more students—Vivian Malone and James Hood—were refused entry by Alabama's governor at the time and a wall of state troopers. Standing there in the oppressive August heat (the massive willow oak trees gave no shade), I took in the names of all three, now etched in the memorial that bears their name. For the second time in my life, the profound sense of sheer wonder rushed through me. Reaching out for Lucy's name reproduced the feelings I had so exactly when I was ten that I almost turned looking for my father's hand.

The night he took me to *Star Wars*, there was simply no chance of either of us being turned away at the ticket booth. There were no back entrances, special seating, or separate washrooms to degrade us. No one would beat my father with a bat or chain, and no policeman would use a cattle-prod on me. My sisters would not be tormented at their school. My mother would not lose her job. No one would shoot at our cars, dynamite our home, or run us out of town. In fact, no one in the community had any fear of being beaten within an inch of their life, or branded, or lynched, or castrated.

This was not the reality for millions of African Americans. Change the theater to anything—grocery store, diner, school, playground, beach, or even a library—and the complete lack of human empathy is as staggering as the unimaginable levels of courage displayed by those who sought to change it.

Autherine Lucy never became a librarian, but a *New York Post* reporter who saw her try wrote, "What is this extraordinary resource of this otherwise unhappy country that it breeds such dignity in its victims."[1] He "watched in awe" as she barely left the campus alive that day. I felt that same awe decades later, standing where she stood.

This book is dedicated to Autherine Lucy, who was denied her life's promise. At great personal cost, she opened the doors for so many others. I think of her often in my career and try to honor her as I practice librarianship.

Acknowledgments

This book would not have been possible without the kindness and generosity of spirt of numerous people, beginning with the veterans of the Civil Rights Movement. I have been deeply moved, inspired, and changed by the time and memories the following people shared with me: Shirley Bates, Melba Pattillo Beals, Clayborne Carson, John Elliot Churchville, Dennis Coleman, Sanderia Faye, Laura Foner, William Hanson, Bruce Hartford, Peter Kellman, Millard Lowe, Patti Miller, Richard Morrisroe, Denise Nicholas, Pattie Mae McDonald, Willie James McDonald, Gwendolyn Zohara Simmons, Sue Sojourner, Sheldon Stromquist, Maria Varela, Ellen Wolfe, and Sarai G. Zitter. Special thanks also belongs to Eve Pomerance, who shared memories and documents of her mother, Sally Belfrage.

Patterson Toby Graham and Karen Cook introduced me to Freedom Libraries and have been kind enough to answer many questions. Special thanks to Dr. Cook for sharing her doctoral thesis with me. I owe much to the University of Alabama, especially professors Jeff Weddle and Elizabeth Aversa. Beth Riggs went the extra mile to ensure I felt Alabama was my second my home. Nancy Derums, Lance Day, Stephanie Ford, Amber Brookins, and Natalie Valente of the BGE are owed particular thanks, as well as everyone belonging to the Lucky Seven.

Debts of gratitude are also owed to my professional colleagues, especially Ursula Brigl, Deanne Perrault, and Karin von Wittgenstein. Dave Clark's praise has never gone unnoticed. Additional thanks go to Barry Coulter at the Daily Townsman, who let me cover the book beat for more than a decade. Both Ian Cobb and Carrie Schafer at e-know.ca also deserve recognition for publishing my work. All of you have helped me stretch and grow as a writer.

I am forever grateful to my parents and my sisters for a lifetime of love and encouragement. My sons, Simon and Daniel, and granddaughter, Harmony, have always and continue to bring joy to my heart and life. Maggie Muir Tuck helped shape my intellect and character decades ago, and there isn't enough thanks to give her.

Catherine Murphy and James Marquand—two documentary filmmakers—also have my gratitude. Catherine opened many doors for me, and poor James searched high and low for a photo of his father at Selma, which was never found. Both were enthusiastic about this book; many, many thanks.

I am especially grateful to my editor, Charles Harmon, whose belief in this book helped shape the final product. His commitment and encouragement to me is another debt I cannot pay.

Of course, the largest debt is owed to Heather, the love of my life and best friend, whose belief in me and support have been immeasurable.

Introduction

It was the crying that woke her.

Twelve-year-old Shirley Ann McDonald had just fallen asleep when the loud wails startled her awake. They were coming from her brother Walter, who, still just a baby, needed to be changed. Shirley Ann stumbled into his room, changed him, and went back to her own bed. Seconds later, bullets crashed into Walter's room, blasting apart his tiny crib. He was unharmed. After she had changed his diaper, Shirley Ann had taken him back to her own room with her, hoping he would sleep better. His sister's concern for her baby brother unwittingly saved his life.

The McDonald home was fired on just before midnight on Wednesday, September 1, 1965. News accounts reported, "The blasts tore through the living room wall and ledge. More blasts from a shotgun ripped through the bedroom where Mrs. McDonald slept with her husband Leon."[1] It remains astounding no one was hurt, as all ten children of the McDonalds were home that night. The shots came from guns wielded by "nightriders"—nocturnal terrorists officially known as the Ku Klux Klan. While this type of racial violence was not new to the citizens of Hayneville, the Civil Rights Movement had seriously increased its occurrence. Because Pattie Mae McDonald supported the movement, she and her family had been the targets of the harassing phone calls and anonymous death threats that were typical of the time.

The attempted murder of her family on that fateful night was thought to be in retaliation for Patti Mae's insistence in housing civil rights workers. Except here the Klan had it wrong. The McDonald home didn't house any civil rights workers at all. It did, however, house something that was crucial to the Civil Rights Movement.

Pattie Mae McDonald operated a "Freedom Library" out of two rooms of her modest home. This was enough to earn her and her family terror and attempted murder.

FREEDOM LIBRARIES

Freedom Libraries were originally a product of "Freedom Summer"—the voting registration campaign launched by various civil rights organizations in Mississippi during the summer of 1964. They were not contained to the Magnolia State, though, and Freedom Libraries appeared throughout the Deep South, and even as far north as Philadelphia. While the Student Nonviolent Coordinating Committee (SNCC) would play a part in establishing a large number of these libraries, some were created by people not affiliated with any official organization. Local citizens including mothers and grandmothers simply saw a need and filled it, no longer expecting the society they lived in to do so.

Information about these libraries has been extremely limited, so much so that their very existence remains "virtually unknown even within the American library community."[2] Five decades of Civil Rights literature barely mentions them, while histories of American libraries ignore them altogether.

Numerous reasons exist for their overlooked nature, including vagaries of memory, lack of surviving documents, and the unfortunate but true fact that "libraries are generally ignored by historians of all kinds . . . used but effectively invisible."[3] Yet as this book will show, Freedom Libraries were extremely critical in supporting the Civil Rights Movement. In fact, libraries in and of themselves were the spine that the whole movement rested on.

This book is the story of the Freedom Libraries—what they were, who created them, why they were needed, and how they supported the human struggle against the overwhelming forces of white supremacy. No two libraries were alike; they ranged from well-stocked rented buildings to basements, attics, and shacks holding whatever books the community could get. While historians may have overlooked them, hostile forces such as the Ku Klux Klan and the Citizens' Council did not. Many of them were bombed, set ablaze, and shot at. Intimidation and threats of (and actual) violence were sadly commonplace for all those involved.

The story of the Freedom Libraries unfolds using both primary and secondary sources, along with interviews and testimony from movement veterans. News clippings, magazine articles, field reports, meeting minutes, personal diaries, incident reports, book lists, and surviving letters have been used to piece together the key events and day-to-day operation of the Freedom Libraries.

Chapter 1 examines the collision of the Civil Rights Movement with the American Public Library. It gives a brief overview of why the publicly funded institutions that were supposed to be "for all" failed to do just that, and why people struggling for their freedom rights were continually denied access to libraries.

Chapters 2 and 3 discuss the 1964 summer program of Mississippi—often known as Freedom Summer—with the movement's intent to create Freedom Libraries. Chapter 4 continues the story of Mississippi and the tragic consequences faced by those who sought to help the state's disenfranchised to realize their right to vote, education, and library service.

Chapter 5 briefly illustrates the historical context of Alabama library service, and the extreme dangers faced by those who challenged the white supremacy. It also explores the 1965 Freedom Library created in Selma and how the workers unintentionally created the largest and best-used library in the area. It also examines the violent consequences that occurred in and around Pattie McDonald's Freedom Library in Hayneville.

Chapter 6 looks at a completely different type of Freedom Library. It isn't in the South, it isn't sponsored by the SNCC, and the people behind it were not interested in an integrated society. Yet the library shares the exact purpose and objectives of its southern counterparts, even if it is surrounded by a different rhetoric.

Chapter 7 charts SNCC's efforts to open and maintain Freedom Libraries in Arkansas—a state that did not want agitation for civil rights in any form, fearing a repeat of 1957's Central High Crisis. While the staff and volunteers were more seasoned by the time they entered Arkansas, they were also facing an organizational shift in policy that became untenable to many.

Chapter 8 traces the impact the Freedom Libraries have had on the Civil Rights Movement, as well as on librarianship, and what their legacy means today.

"The American people are infected with racism—that is the peril," Dr. King told *Look* magazine in 1968. "Paradoxically, they are also infected with democratic ideals—that is the hope."[4] American libraries were born out of the twin ideals of democracy and hope; Freedom Libraries were their finest embodiment.

Chapter One

━━━━━━━━━━━━━━━━━━◯━━━━━━━━━━━━━━━━━━

The American Public Library Meets the Civil Rights Movement

KING WAS lucky.

In the spring of 1938, a young boy handed two books across a large desk to a librarian, along with his library card. This was the second part of a familiar rite of passage that played out in libraries all across the United States (and continues today). Many milestones in young people's lives help initiate them into the adult world, none more important than a library card all one's own. Besides ownership and thoughtful responsibility, the card allows children to make their own choices, explore the larger world around them, and—more often than not—help discover who they are inside.

Martin Luther King Jr. was only nine when he passed the books along with his card for checkout. This was at Atlanta's Auburn Avenue Branch Library, and King was an absolute regular there. Not only did he live on the same street as the library, but also his home was less than two blocks away. That the precocious nine-year-old interested in reading and big words lived so close to a library is almost too perfect. That the two books he sought to check out that day were both about Gandhi is astounding.[1]

But there was a hiccup.

After looking at the books and the card, the librarian told King he was not allowed to check these books out. History doesn't record either person's reaction, but the librarian's strong "no" may have been said with a wink. The Gandhi books were restricted to adult

1

card holders only, but if he brought in his father's library card, she would be happy to check out the books to him.

Annie L. McPheeters was the name of the woman willing to bend if not break the rules for her young patron, where she had been the branch's director since 1936. Of course, this was still Atlanta's segregated library.[2]

NOT FOR ALL

Andrew Carnegie had built an architecturally impressive public library, also Atlanta's first, in 1902. Carnegie's "free for all" motto would not apply to Atlanta's African American populations, who nonetheless paid taxes to support it.

W. E. B. Du Bois, a professor of sociology at Atlanta University, lobbied the library board to try and actually make it "free for all." He was not successful, with the board responding, "Negroes would not be permitted to use the Carnegie Library in Atlanta." The board tried to appease Du Bois with promises of a "separate but equal" branch library, but when they refused to have African American representation on the board, Du Bois realized where their hearts lay. The board did secure funding and would open the segregated branch on Auburn Avenue, but not until 1921—enough time for a full generation to come of age without any library service available to them.[3]

"Segregated," "Negro," or "colored" libraries throughout the United States were typically afterthoughts—underfunded shacks or abandoned buildings with a minimal collection of useless castoffs, operated by an untrained staff.

McPheeters succeeded in spite of these constraints, transforming the Auburn Avenue Branch into a useable and responsive public library. She secured grant money from the American Association of Adult Education and the Julius Rosenwald Fund. She initiated an adult education program, engaged in community outreach, and started a comprehensive collection dedicated to Negro History, often using her own money to purchase much-needed materials. She also made sure curious nine-year-olds could read about Gandhi if they wanted to.[4]

As mentioned above, King was lucky.

Millions of African Americans did not share this reality. For them, public library service was nonexistent. None of this was as it should have been, but the spread and growth of publicly funded libraries across the country after the Reconstruction Era regrettably parallels the spread and growth of a brutal and extreme hatred.

PUBLIC LIBRARY BEGINNINGS

The American Public Library Movement was born on October 14, 1852. This was when the city council of Boston, Massachusetts, ratified *City Document* 37, which not only created a paradigm for libraries supported by the tax dollars of those who use them but also mandated "free admission for all, circulation of books for home use, and the acquisition of reading materials ranging from scholarly to popular."[5]

Boston's *City Document* 37 quickly became the blueprint that helped spark the growth of tax-supported public libraries across the United States. The American Library Association was formed not long after in 1876, "for the purpose of promoting library interests by exchanging views, reaching conclusions, and inducing cooperation in all departments of bibliothecal science and economy; by disposing the public mind to the founding and improving of libraries; and by cultivating good will among its own members."[6]

These two forces helped expand and establish public libraries across the nation. While this included services to the poor and foreign born, the majority of African Americans were simply and strategically denied access to them. Again, none of this was as it should have been. The Thirteenth (dissolution of slavery), Fourteenth, (African Americans are American citizens), and Fifteenth (all citizens may vote regardless of race) Amendments all but guaranteed the erosion of differences between the races.

Southern politicians didn't see it this way, embracing and enforcing an unreconstructed way of life that enforced white supremacy first by custom, then by law. The idea that "blackness was contamination" permeated daily life, and fictional "separate but equal" public spaces reinforced this debased belief.[7]

THE CRUELEST ACT

The familiar examples of the white/colored drinking fountains, the back of the bus seating, and separate washrooms are only part of the story, as segregation ruled over schools, hospitals, cemeteries, grocery stores, hair salons, department stores, ice cream stands, zoos, restaurants, nightclubs, ballparks, playgrounds, elevators, parking lots, theaters, phone booths, sporting events, and of course libraries. Without seeking to minimize or discount the cruel and inhuman effects of all this, the segregation of a public library is a different animal altogether.

No amusement park is necessary for democracy to work, and no waiting area was created so citizens could learn, advance, and thrive as informed citizens. The American public library is, among many things, a "monument to democracy," a "beacon of hope," a "tangible representative of humanity's ideals," and "the single most important institution in America." The intentional denial of library service has to be one of the cruelest acts of Jim Crow. This may be the very reason why the library itself would loom large during the Civil Rights Movement—becoming either a target of protests or a meeting place for activists to plan and regroup.[8]

It wasn't just that the libraries were segregated. Librarians in the South filled their children's collections with literature conforming to their blatant hatred of African Americans, ensuring the youngest of minds would be indoctrinated. From picture books up to readers for young teens, these works portrayed a "stubborn, yet aggressive, racial ideology of white superiority, privilege, and black subservience."[9] The fact that so much hate literature was churned out by writers is as disheartening as it is sickening. That librarians actively sought these authors remains one of the most shameful acts in the profession's history.

CIVIL RIGHTS BEGINNINGS

It was in May of 1954 when the Supreme Court ruled that separate but equal schools were unconstitutional, which—although setting off a hostile and often violent backlash—may have been the beginning of the end of denying a large portion of American citizens their freedom rights. Rosa Parks was arrested for not changing bus seats the following year, and it was not long until four North Carolina college students refused to leave the Woolworth's lunch counter after being refused service. This "sit-in" was soon replicated by others in cities all across the southern states.

The direct-action combination of nonviolence with civil disobedience of the sit-in demonstrations appealed to those wishing to desegregate libraries. What became known as the "read-in" movement is stated to have begun on April 2, 1960, when a dozen high school students in Danville, Virginia, were refused service at that city's public library. The students filed a lawsuit against the city, and a federal judge ordered the library to immediately desegregate. The city responded to the federal court order by closing the library. Finding themselves quickly back in court, the city claimed the library closed due to being "overtaxed." Not amused and "unconvinced by the charade," the court ordered Danville to reopen their library and desegregate it.[10]

"Oh mercy, Miss Scoggin, there's colored people all over the library!"—was heard at another Virginia library, but this was two decades before the Danville ruling. On a warm morning in August 1939, five well-dressed African American men entered the Alexandria Public Library and politely requested library cards. Upon refusal, each man pulled a book off various shelves and sat down to read. The police arrived and asked the men to leave. Upon refusal, all five were arrested for disorderly conduct. These charges were later dismissed, as the arresting officers could not testify to disorderly anything by the would-be library users.[11]

This original read-in was directed by a young attorney named Samuel Wilbert Tucker. The short route from his home to his office each day had him pass the Alexandria Public Library, a place he would never be allowed in. Months before his five cohorts were arrested, he had tried to get his own library card, but was refused. He filed a petition against the city in court, but this was stalled and postponed at every turn, until the city agreed to build a segregated library. Tucker was offered a library card stamped "colored," to be used sometime in the future, if and whenever the colored library was built.

This was not what Tucker had in mind. A surviving letter he wrote to Miss Scoggin and the city conveys his feelings: "I refuse and will always refuse to accept a card to be used at [the proposed colored library] . . . in lieu of a card to be used at the existing library."[12]

Things did not go Tucker's way. He had hoped his actions and those of the five arrested men would make national news and thus inspire others; this was not to be. News of the arrests was completely overshadowed by Germany and the Soviet Union signing the Hitler–Stalin Pact on the exact same day. Alexandria did indeed build a segregated branch for African Americans, the expected inferior building with "shorter hours, castoff books, and a hand-me-down typewriter." The Alexandria Public Library would eventually desegregate, but not until 1964.[13]

Although no one may have read about Tucker's actions outside of his hometown, many felt the same way he did. By the time the middle of the twentieth century arrived, a full onslaught of library protests was taking place all across the South, right up to, and some past, the appearance of Freedom Libraries. (See table 1.1 for a timeline of African American library events.)

DEVASTATING EVIDENCE

The beating of the two Anniston ministers was "one of the most disturbing events in the history of American public libraries";[14] it was also quite telling of what the future would bring. The more African Americans tried to use the libraries that their taxes paid for, the greater the white resistance would be. The intimidation, terror, and brutal violence were met with some of the most uncommon and profound courage of those who knew deep down they had every right to read.

This story is not complete without mentioning the conspicuous silence of the American Library Association (ALA)—the largest professional association of U.S. libraries. While against segregation

Table 1.1. Timeline of African American Library Actions

July 26, 1950	Chief librarian Ruth Brown is fired from her job at the Bartlesville, Oklahoma, public library, ostensibly for promoting subversive and communist literature, but in reality, she was dismissed for conducting story times at Bartlesville's segregated library.
July 8, 1954	Army captain and attorney Robert Hainsworth is defeated in the supreme court of Texas after requesting the Houston Law Library be desegregated.
May 22, 1957	A Purcellville, Virginia, interior decorator is refused use of a French drape-making book from the public library, and sues the city (later winning).
July 15, 1957	Montgomery, Alabama, librarian Juliet Morgan commits suicide, after receiving countless death threats and having her home vandalized. She had publicly complained that it was untenable that libraries exclude African Americans.
August 28, 1958	The NAACP files a lawsuit against the city of Memphis after a prominent bank employee is refused entrance into the public library.
October 22, 1959	The Savannah, Georgia, public library board turns down a formal request for African Americans to use the white-only library.
December 17, 1959	After learning that the public library board had no intention of desegregating the library as promised, two Portsmouth, Virginia, dentists file a lawsuit against them.
March 22, 1960	Thirty-eight African Americans are arrested in Memphis after attempting to use the all-white library.
April 4, 1960	The library "should not cause the humiliation to Petersburg's Negro citizens," states Virginia McKenney Claiborne, who demands that the city desegregate immediately. Claiborne's wishes carried some weight, as her father had donated the library property to the city.
September 19, 1960	A district court judge orders the Greenville, South Carolina, library to reopen and integrate. The library had been closed for weeks after seven African American students tried to use it.
March 27, 1961	Medgar Evers is violently beaten by police after his support of the nine students from Tougaloo College arrested for staging a sit-in at the public library in Jackson, Mississippi.

(continued)

Table 1.1. *(continued)*

May 25, 1961	The American Library Association adopts a resolution stating they are against segregated libraries, although they did so without any input from or consultation with African American librarians.
August 17, 1961	A Memphis, Tennessee, district court judge orders the toilets at the library to be desegregated, despite the insistence by the library board that "venereal disease is much higher among Negroes."
April 23, 1962	After being ordered to desegregate, officials at the Montgomery, Alabama, public library remove all the tables and chairs, enforcing "vertical integration."
May 22, 1962	Chief librarian John Uhler quits his job in Plaquemine, Louisiana, after the city orders him "not to make library services available to Negroes under any circumstances."
July 12, 1962	Four Greenville, Mississippi, students are denied use of the white library after requesting permission from city council to do so. The students had hoped the city would quietly desegregate in order to "combat racial problems before they affect the peace and harmony of the community."
August 2, 1962	Albany, Georgia, police padlock the city library to prevent African Americans from gaining entrance.
March 11, 1963	Albany, Georgia, officials remove padlocks off of the library, but also remove all chairs and tables. Their reference room remains closed to African Americans.
April 11, 1963	A handful of African Americans successfully enter the Birmingham Public Library, even though they are told to go home because they stink.
July 25, 1963	After being refused library cards at the white library, seven Columbus, Georgia, teenagers are arrested.
August 1, 1963	The American Library Association reports that racial bias in Washington, DC, libraries is as bad as it is in Birmingham, Alabama.
August 2, 1963	The police in Pine Bluff, Arkansas, haul off twenty-five African Americans to jail for picketing outside the city's public library.
September 15, 1963	Two Anniston, Alabama, ministers are "knifed, chain-whipped, and savagely beaten" by a large mob after they try to enter the public library.

on paper, the ALA took zero action to help anyone integrate the libraries. "When a book is banned in the smallest hamlet, there is a vigorous protest," wrote an ALA member from New York. "But when a city takes away the right of citizens to read every book in the public library, we say nothing."[15] One wonders if the beatings experienced by the two Anniston ministers could have been avoided if the ALA had taken action much sooner.

In December of 1963, the U.S. Commission on Civil Rights published its investigation into southern libraries. It was full of what the commission called "devastating evidence" of what everyone already knew: that "two thirds of the Negro population of 13 Southern States were entirely without library services," and that "nearly 10 million Negro citizens of our land are totally or partially denied access to publicly owned books." The commission found barring African Americans from libraries was "an indefensible act of discrimination," and "absurd." They were even less amused by the "lack of cooperation and open hostility of the State and local Officials." The commission concluded, "Surely . . . these discriminations violate the Federal law. . . . Surely they also violate the equal protection clause."[16]

These "discriminations" did indeed violate federal laws, but—as discussed above—people with the power to do something stuck their head in the sand, either out of apathy or quietly hoping it would all just go away. It was around this time that the young nine-year-old who wanted to read books about Gandhi would (now an adult) discuss at length "the appalling silence of good people." He wasn't specifically talking about libraries, but they were certainly included.[17]

It was not going to all just go away. Up north, in the small Ohio town of Oxford, there was a group of people—mostly young—who were planning a full-on assault on the southern states. They would do so with their bodies, their sheer numbers, and their courage.

They would also do it with books.

Chapter Two

———————◯———————

Mississippi
The People without Books

SHERRY ZITTER was angry.

It was a short walk for Sherry Zitter from her home to her grade 6 class at Ridge Road School in Cedar Grove, New Jersey. The trek was a bit longer one morning in the spring of 1964, as the eleven-year-old was dragging a large cardboard box with her. On the side of the box she had written "BOOKS FOR MISSISSIPPI NEGRO CHILDREN." Civil rights workers had put the call out for book donations, which were badly needed for the Freedom Schools and Libraries being set up in Mississippi. Sherry could not imagine growing up without anything to read, so she immediately created a donation box. Her teacher let her address the class, knowing that Sherry's desire to help was probably in her genes.[1]

Both her parents were activists. While her father spent his free time picketing the South African embassy in the fight against apartheid, her mother started Cedar Grove's Fair Housing Committee out of their living room, in response to property value complaints after an interracial couple had bought a home there. Her mother was also a member of CORE (Congress on Racial Equality), which is where both she and her daughter learned about the call for books, causing Sherry to drag the oversized box to her school.[2]

She "made an impassioned plea to her sixth-grade class" to donate books to kids who didn't have any. By the end of the week, the box was virtually empty. As her hope turned to rage, she blasted her classmates for their indifference.[3]

It has never been easy to get books to Mississippi.

RACE DIFFERENCE

The state had had it rough—especially during the first half of the twentieth century. "The South today is the most rural section in the United States," surmised economist Wilson Gee in 1924. "[And] the most rural state in the Nation is Mississippi." The southern states also had the lowest income in the country, with—again—Mississippi having the lowest income of any state. With no money to spend on educational facilities, illiteracy became widespread. All this led Gee to conclude that "the rural South is a backward South."[4]

Three decades later not much had changed. A study by educators in 1952 found the Magnolia State continued to spend "less per capita for the education of its citizens, that it has the poorest school facilities, and that it hires teachers with less training than any other state." A vicious circle existed where education was the way out of poverty, but that very poverty created no tax base to fund opportunities for education.[5]

Much was to blame for Mississippi's overwhelmingly poor condition on all fronts, including confusion and disorganization after the Civil War, the refusal of federal government aid and intervention, and the increase of tenant farming. But it was the state's commitment to Jim Crow that was the real reason for being ranked last. The Supreme Court ruling of *Plessy v. Ferguson* of 1896, which stated separate but equal public facilities were more than acceptable for African Americans, not only created legal justification for these "permissions to hate," but also would insidiously delay the state's progress.[6]

Mary U. Rothrock—a librarian from Knoxville, Tennessee, and future ALA president—saw this clearly. "So, in 1865," she told a captive audience at the forty-fifth annual meeting of the American Library Association in Hot Springs, Arkansas, "the Southern states, with a severely depleted population, empty treasuries, with governmental organizations which lacked the confidence of the public, faced the necessity of building up, not one educational system alone, but two, one for the white and another for the Negro population."[7]

Rothrock's sentiments were echoed by others at the meeting. The director of the North Carolina Library Commission, Mary B. Palmer, knew this situation had caused the general "booklessness" of the South, because "provision must always be made for separate service." Palmer felt library development was constrained by "poverty, ignorance, and race difference."[8]

The Hot Springs Conference concluded with a brief mention of ALA's newly formed Work with Negroes Round Table. "Reaching the Negro" was the most immediate topic, admitting that library service for African Americans was poor in all states. It also recognized what it called "the Louisville way" of library service, the separate segregated library. The round table somehow washed its hands of any commitment, stating, "We are not here to advocate separate libraries or mixed libraries."[9]

And this was the good news coming out of the conference. Condescending attitudes still blocked any progress, from the well-meaning "educated and refined colored girls are the same stuff as white" to the arrogant "the so-called higher capacities . . . are decidedly less efficient than whites." This last "scientific fact" was preventing the librarian from the New Orleans Public Library from knowing which books to select for his segregated branches. African Americans' "mental training and lack of culture" were making his job difficult.[10]

A dozen years later, not much had changed. "Measured by any index involving library resources, the circulation of magazines and newspapers, the presence of book stores and rental libraries, the rural South ranks far below all other sections," concluded Dr. Louis R. Wilson, president of the ALA, in 1937. Once again, ranking below all states was Mississippi. What little help the lower per capita income of the state contributed was further reduced because education and library service "must be provided for two races." Wilson also was comfortable stating that "the service to Negroes has not been developed on an equal basis."[11]

Those he spoke to felt "book learning," Wilson reported, "as distinguished from schooling, for the Negro is not essential." Eighty-three percent of all African Americans were without library service of any kind. The remaining 17 percent could only access collections that were not only "meager and badly worn," but also "not carefully chosen as they should be to meet the requirements of those for whom they were made available."[12]

PEOPLE WITHOUT BOOKS

"The libraries of Mississippi are weak in books, are poorly housed, and lack trained personnel: the demands made upon them by citizens are beyond their capacity. Few of them are prepared to give the type of library service which every citizen may reasonably expect."[13] This was the incriminatory conclusion of the University of Mississippi's Bureau of Public Administration in 1949, after their yearlong survey of the state's library services. The causes of these dismal findings were the same culprits mentioned above: poverty ("If the economics status is so low that people are forced to devote all their time to procuring the necessary food and clothing, they are not likely to give thought to school, clubs, or libraries"), illiteracy ("Before a demand for library service can develop, the people in the area must be able to read"), and race ("Most libraries serve only the white population. . . . No [rural] facilities are offered to serve the colored half of the population").[14] With no current efforts to correct this situation, the survey demonstrated that Mississippi truly was what the survey's title said it was: people without books.

There was hope, though.

The Mississippi Library Commission took the People without Books report very seriously. This had to change. The commission lobbied tirelessly for change in legislation that would provide much more governmental support for both urban and rural libraries. The state's change of property tax law in 1952 was a welcomed result of the commission's lobbying.[15]

Congress's Library Services Act of 1956, intent on providing "extension of public library services in rural areas without such services or with inadequate services," gave Mississippi an extra $40,000 per year for the following five years. While Mississippi would use this money to greatly expand library service, by 1957 there were still over a million residents without it. Even by the end of their five-year Library Services Act grant, they still found that "no library service in the state reaches anything like national standards."[16]

But the commission had done so much with so little. In fact, Mississippi quickly became known for its shoestring approach to library service all over the world. The State Department began to receive international requests to visit their rural libraries. Foreign library delegates from Pakistan, India, South Africa, and even New Zealand were all given tours of Mississippi's most remote public libraries. This is an incredible example of truly global collaboration, which even predates the study of comparative librarianship.[17]

No record has been kept on whether or not the delegates noticed that African Americans weren't allowed anywhere near the libraries they were touring (it should be noted that the delegates came from countries that had their own caste systems, so they either may not have noticed, or expected to find it that way).

SHARING BOOKS WITH WHITE PEOPLE

Although the Library Services Act grant gave the Mississippi Library Commission "broad discretion as to where and how it should be spent—and for what," money from the state itself was not so flexible. The state's legislature would disburse $109,650 on the condition that $5,000 of it be "used for the purchase of books dealing with the subject of ethnology." The term *ethnology* was just a fancier one for white supremacy ideology. The Library Commission wasn't alone with this stipulation; the state's school curricula bill was to include "ethnology" as well.[18]

The ethnology requirement didn't sit well with other members of government. Governor James P. Coleman vetoed that part of the bill, citing, "There are just not enough books of this type available so as to justify the expenditure." Representative Joel Blass was also against it, strongly objecting to anyone mandating what the Library

Commission should or should not buy. Senator Flavous Lambert felt it was "contrary to the democratic principles to dictate what the commission should buy," and that it would "hamstring the commission."[19]

The director of the Mississippi Library Commission was opposed to the ethnology requirement as well. Lura G. Currier, who was appointed in 1957, passively fought against it, spending only $200 on ethnology, and the other $4,800 on actual anthropology books written by actual scientists. Currier remains a curious paradox in librarianship. Her actions regarding library service to African Americans remain questionable at best; she appears to be one of those "white moderates" whose actions did more harm than good. Freedom Libraries were necessary in Mississippi in no small part because of her (although she would offer them help when they did arrive).[20]

Prior to her directorship, Currier worked as a teacher, a journalist, a consultant, and a much-in-demand speaker. She was also extremely active in both the Mississippi Library Association and its parent body, the American Library Association. Her struggle to be of service to all residents of Mississippi became clear when the ALA decided to expel any state chapters practicing segregation. Mississippi chose expulsion, although Currier was very much displeased with this decision.

She felt the decision by the ALA was a vindictive one that in no way helped the states that continued to have segregated libraries. She also felt that this was the time when the states needed the ALA and its leadership more than ever. She appeared to feel that since the Civil Rights Movement had forced organizations to take a hard look at themselves, the ALA "felt it necessary to cleanse itself of us because of conditions which were not created by librarians and which cannot possibly be solved by them." Although the ALA was somewhat perplexed by her response, Currier was not alone in her feelings. There were many who felt ALA's stance on this issue was going to create more problems than it would solve (in fact, this is exactly how the ALA felt not long before this).[21]

Currier had also worked hard for and supported the segregated library system of her state. She rationalized this by adopting the stance of working within the system instead of trying to change it. "Access to libraries" was her concern, believing the only way to do this for African Americans was through the continuation of segregated branches. She backed up this position by stating that African Americans told her they appreciated some library service, as opposed to none if they waited to "share books with white people."[22]

Where to begin?

The hurt Currier and others felt at the ALA's mandate remains completely inconsequential to the hurt of daily life in Mississippi's Jim Crow society. Segregated anything—let alone libraries—remains one of the worst nightmares of the twentieth century. Her comments about appreciative users of the segregated libraries utterly fails to take into account the fact that African Americans adopted a submissive, deferential, and ultimately demeaning "yes ma'am" attitude as a means of daily survival.[23]

While she admonished the ALA for lack of leadership, where was hers? She was the director of the MLC, a thoughtful teacher, an elegant writer, and a popular speaker ("Enthralling audiences is not unusual for Lura Currier").[24]

She was hardly alone in this, though. There were many people positioned to effect change who chose not to. Alabama, Louisiana, and Georgia library chapters also chose expulsion from the ALA rather than desegregation of their libraries. The ALA Bulletin voiced concern that only "harm and ill will" would result from the ALA "overtly interfering in a local situation." This was echoed by southern librarians who felt "statements by outside agencies such as ALA will do more harm than good because they are deeply resented and further inflame already hot tempers."[25]

The logic of this is astounding. The daily lives of African Americans were already "deeply resented." Their basic existence already "further inflamed" the white society they lived in. There wasn't a statement or action that the ALA could make that would ever worsen the "disease of racism" that "affected and damaged" every African American. "Harm and ill will" were already a constant factor of daily life.[26]

These weren't the only obstacles African Americans faced. Something more dangerous was happening.

ESPECIALLY FOR CHILDREN

On Sunday, February 21, 1960, the Mississippi Department of Eight and Forty presented a complete set of *World Book* encyclopedias to the state preventorium (the children's ward of the tuberculosis sanatorium just outside the town of McGee). The books were a gift from the World Book Company to the Eight and Forty (a veterans' service organization). A photographer from the *Clarion-Ledger* was on hand, snapping a photo of two young patients displaying the newly donated books. Among the women photographed during this presentation ceremony was a Mrs. Sara McCorkle, listed as the L'Avocate for the preventorium.[27]

This was typical of McCorkle, who by all accounts did everything she could for the young people of Mississippi. She was head of numerous organizations, including the Government Program of Girls State, the American Legion Auxiliary, Patriotic American Youth, and various iterations of Parent Teacher Advisories across the state. McCorkle was very much a book person, sponsoring and reviewing books for both public and school libraries, working closely with publishers and distributors such as the World Book Company, as well as sponsoring high school literary contests, which would award a $500 college scholarship to the author of the best entry. She also averaged about a dozen speaking engagements per week, not just to schools, but also to women's clubs and civic organizations. She received the Hinds County Bar Association's Liberty Bell Award in 1970 for her work. On September 11, 1986, Mississippi governor Bill Allain declared it was Sara McCorkle Day across the state, the occasion marked by her ninetieth birthday.[28]

This last accolade would probably not appear the oddest of the bunch if McCorkle hadn't achieved all she did on the backs of, and at the expense of, African Americans. Her tireless work for youth was strictly for the cause of white supremacy. The one organization she vigorously put all her efforts into was the White Citizens' Council, a hate group comprised of white-collar community leaders, unofficially known as the "Uptown Klan."[29]

Her contacts with the World Book Company are telling. McCorkle and the council were highly offended by the *N* volume of the encyclopedia, which defined the term *Negro* as "loosely to mean a member of the Negroid group, but no sharp line can be drawn between the so-called 'races.' . . . Negroid physical traits are also found among other racial groups." Demeaning claims of this sort deeply offended the White Citizens' Council, who concluded it had to have been penned by a "professional agitator." An expose of this wrongdoing titled *Especially for Children: Grandpa's World Book Exposed* claimed the encyclopedia's publisher had grandfathered an African American, wrote a book "outright plugging for the destruction of the American way of life," and supported a host of other pro–civil rights causes.[30]

Did McCorkle excise the offending passage on *Negro* while donating the set to the state preventorium? It is more than probable that she did. Appointed as chief censor of the White Citizens' Council, she arbitrated over library books, school texts, and any and all material for the slightest hint of racial equality, which included the Anti-Defamation League's *High Wall* filmstrip, and the toy Playtime Farm (whose toy figure of the farmer was shaded slightly too dark for his white wife).

"Why I Believe in Social Separation of the Races of Mankind," "Subversion of Racial Unrest," "Why Separate Schools Should Be Maintained for the White and Negro Races," and "Why the Preservation of States Rights Is Important to Every American" were among the topics high school students could write about for McCorkle's $500 scholarship prize. Interested applicants would receive a list of topics, a selection of carefully curated books to use, and a thank-you letter. The letter was stamped with an image of an American soldier "kicking a white girl of grammar school age in the head and forcing her nose against that of a negro girl of the same age."[31]

A "pretty coed from Hattiesburg High" would win first prize that year.[32]

McCorkle was also instrumental in reaching the youngest of minds, distributing a series of primary readers to elementary schools. Easy readers that taught essential life lessons such as "Negros are lazy" and "God wanted the white people to live alone" were imparted with these White Citizens' Council–produced readers.[33]

"I have always loved young people," McCorkle told a reporter for the *Clarion-Ledger* in 1982. "I have always sought their companionship. I have listened to them intently because they are the most brilliant group I've ever been associated with." For a woman so committed to instilling racial injustice and anti-intellectualism into impressionable minds, her definition of *love* is nothing short of bizarre.[34]

This would leave the last line of hope for African Americans with the librarians themselves.

Many found themselves conflicted—in Mississippi segregation was both tradition and law—one that was all too frequently brutally enforced.

To desegregate the libraries of Mississippi, to support the state's most disadvantaged citizens, and to admit that Mississippi was actually "part of the United States of America . . . [where] blacks too enjoyed the rights of American citizens" were all actions Currier and others truly believed were "completely out of the province of librarians."[35]

Not everyone felt this way, including Bob Moses.

THE STUDENT NONVIOLENT COORDINATING COMMITTEE

Mississippi—really, the entirety of the southern states—was not ready for Bob Moses. Arriving in the summer of 1961, Moses represented the Student Nonviolent Coordinating Committee (SNCC) and had entered the state to initiate direct action, the kind the Civil Rights Movement was becoming famous for.

In mid-August of that year, Moses was arrested for assisting three local residents in their attempt to register to vote. Charged with "interfering with an officer in the discharge of his duties," Moses was brought to the city jail and offered his one phone call. He did not call any of his local contacts for bail, or anyone from the SNCC. Instead he placed a collect call to the U.S. Department of Justice in Washington, DC, and asked for John Doar (President Kennedy's deputy assistant attorney general). Doar's acceptance of Moses's collect call spread confusion in his arresting officers, slightly cracking the insular fiction Mississippi law enforcement felt was their birthright.[36]

The following week, Moses once again returned to the courthouse to assist others through the registration process. This time he was badly beaten on the sidewalk just outside the courthouse. Concussed and bloody, Moses insisted they continue, but the stunned registrar inside quickly closed for the day. The following day, Moses appeared at the county attorney's office, wishing to file a complaint against his assailant, somehow believing he was a citizen of the United States, which entitled him not to be beaten. The results were little more than a show trial, with his white assailant being easily acquitted as incensed white supremacists fired off shotguns outside the court.[37]

Moses had been in Mississippi less than a month.

It would be his relationship with Amzie Moore that would kick off the high-water mark of the Civil Rights Movement. A business owner and president of a local NAACP chapter, it was Moore himself who had convinced Moses a year earlier to bring his considerable talents to Mississippi. What African Americans needed more than anything was the vote, Moore felt. Only full and equal participation in the political process would produce the results they both sought. Moses had not considered this initially, believing the direct action of sit-ins and boycotts was what was needed.

Following Moore's lead, Moses hinted that the SNCC could recruit a small army of young people to help with organizing and canvassing for voter drives and registration. Moore suggested something else entirely. Instead of a small army of locals from within, what was needed was a large army from without. "It would be better," he told Moses, "for SNCC to send a work force of students into Mississippi to register voters."[38]

What history would call Freedom Summer was born right there and then, and Moses was to be the chief architect of it. Over one thousand volunteers of mostly college-aged whites would invade Mississippi in the summer of 1964. They would form one of the most ambitious voting drive efforts the state had ever experienced, as well as set up supporting efforts such as health clinics, legal help, and education. That most of them were white was critical and on purpose. It was the only way to get news media to pay any attention. They would also establish libraries, providing the first meaningful exposure African Americans would have with books. This was important.

"The matter of books and reading marks the experience of black folk in America in a way that is deeply political and resonantly personal," commented Karla F. C. Holloway in an instructive memoir about segregated reading practices. "Blacks in the United States developed an intimate relationship to books because of the way books personify the story of race."[39]

The right to vote would be everything for African Americans. The right to read would be something else entirely. Voting would make them citizens; libraries would make them free.

Moses understood this intuitively, and he began to build a small but functioning collection of books in the SNCC office in the town of Greenwood, in preparation for Freedom Summer. Almost concurrently, David Dennis—the director of CORE, was establishing a library at the CORE headquarters in Canton, just 75 miles south of Greenwood.

Dennis would launch a Books for Mississippi drive in October of 1963. He recognized early on that the terror of Jim Crow produced a marked learned helplessness, which he believed free access to "objective books and information" would combat.[40]

"My suggestion now," Dennis wrote to CORE's National Action Committee, "is to open a center in Mississippi, beginning with a library."[41]

THE LIBRARY PROJECT

A married couple from Brooklyn would set up a third library in Meridian in preparation for the summer of 1964. "My husband and myself are to be responsible for getting the center started," wrote Rita Schwerner to Anne Braden, editor of the *Southern Patriot*. "Before leaving New York City, I was an English teacher and Mike a social worker. I will be doing the teaching and setting up the library. . . . We need books."[42]

Within a month, Mickey and Rita Schwerner would be "up to ears in books." Mickey would report that "the library is truly starting to function and books are being taken out by people in the community." By March they would have received and cataloged ten thousand books. The Schwerners would echo Dennis's conviction regarding the intrinsic value the Freedom Libraries would provide: "Psychologically the center is filling the need among the people for recognition, for a place to come and talk, for something that is for them." This last sentence would be the perfect mission statement of any public library.[43]

On May 4, NOW! *The Voice of Freedom* (the official newsletter of the SNCC) reported on "The Library Project." This write-up stated two volunteers, Larry Rubin and Emmie Schrader, had arrived in Mississippi to begin "the tremendous task of organizing the close to 100,000 books that are presently stored in various places in the state." It also mentioned how Rubin would begin hauling all the books to Rust College.[44]

It did not go this way.

The FBI reported that on May 7, "six volunteer workers for SNCC were arrested in Mississippi for reckless driving, at which time they were hauling books for SNCC." A similar report released by the Council of Federated Organizations (COFO) stated Rubin was originally pulled over for a faulty trailer light. Not only was he "accused of stealing books," but the books themselves were "said to advocate overthrow of Govt."[45]

In a letter to her mother, Emmie Schrader wrote how Rubin had attempted to drive a moving trailer full of books to Rust College "but the cops had a roadblock out for him. He is in jail on charges of carrying subversive literature instigating the people to revolt or some other such claptrap. A trailer load of children's books!" Schrader's concern for her friend took a backseat to her concern for the cargo he was hauling. "I am not so much worried about him, everyone seems to be in and out of jail down here, but am worried that they may destroy the books."[46]

Just how did the Schwerners find themselves "up to their ears" in volumes, and where did the books come from that Rubin was hauling?

Some came from Sherry Zittner, whose vocal indignation toward her classmates had produced results. She soon had a full box of books to ship to Mississippi. And she wasn't the only one. Book drives and collections were an overwhelming success, and soon thousands and thousands of books were being collected and shipped to Mississippi.

In an editorial titled *A Small Band of Practical Heroes*, John Fischer wrote in *Harper's* about Moses and the SNCC's efforts in setting up "a small library for Negroes in Greenwood." The proposed library would like "a good set of reference books, children's books and books written by Negroes." Reminding readers that "Negroes are of course barred from white libraries," Fischer also lists contact and address information for sending books. Fischer's editorial produced a "flood of donated books."[47]

Similar requests were published elsewhere, including *Jet* and the *Southern Patriot,* which was also accompanied by book drives from clergy, lawyers, and business owners. Various universities and colleges, publishers, and libraries also sent books. A report from the COFO office commented that "thousands of gift books were pouring in, from interested people in the North."[48]

The Books for Mississippi project was mentioned by David Dennis in an edition of the *CORE-altor,* thanking Benjamin Brown of the national CORE office, and passing along Brown's own gratitude: "Brown wishes to thank all those individuals and groups having donated books." Dennis also reminded readers of the purpose for all the book-collecting efforts: to support the Freedom Centers and to "offset the effects of economic and cultural deprivation, a place where an attempt can be made to show children and parents that their plight is not normal and that significant change is possible."[49]

Only the libraries in Greenwood and Meridian would greet the Mississippi Project volunteers. The one in Canton was effectively dissolved by that city's White Citizens' Council. The chronic harassment Dennis and other volunteers were under finally peaked when the city had the Freedom House condemned after the police arrested everyone inside. Salvaged items were transferred to Meridian.[50]

Freedom Summer would begin in Mississippi in the third week of June. As the volunteers poured into the state, they would "pit the depth of America's bigotry against the height of America's hope," with the "impassioned insistence that America simply live up to its creed."[51]

As June turned into July, someone knocked on the door of the modest house of Carrie Clayton in Laurel, Mississippi. The knocker was Gwendolyn Robinson, a young Freedom Summer volunteer who had arrived from Atlanta. So far, no one in Laurel had been willing to open their homes to any of the volunteers; fear was as constant as the overbearing summer heat. Hearing the knock, Clayton made her way to the door as quickly as her elderly frame would let her. Upon Clayton opening it, Robinson once again explained who she was, why she was there, and that she was looking for a place to stay. A large smile cracked across Clayton's face. "Girl," she told Robinson, "I've been waiting for you my entire life."[52]

Books had finally come to Mississippi.

Chapter Three

———————————◯———————————

We Are Afraid

The Freedom Libraries

GETTING BOOKS INTO MISSISSIPPI was one thing. For Gwendolyn Robinson, getting herself to Mississippi was quite another. A scholarship student from Atlanta's Spelman College, she was departing for the Freedom Summer Project from the campus when her parents suddenly appeared. Having learned of her plans, they forced her to return to Memphis, locking her in her bedroom and intercepting all her mail and phone calls. Deeply ashamed of their daughter's actions, they told her one day she would thank them for stopping her.[1]

Two years earlier, Robinson had no intention of letting anything distract her college career—what she called "her opportunity of a lifetime." Campus visits by the SNCC (Student Nonviolent Coordinating Committee) and other exposure to the black struggle for freedom rights led her to reexamine her commitment to not engage in protest activities. By the end of her second year, Robinson was a board member of the SNCC, helped organize and participate in marches and sit-ins, and was arrested and jailed twice. Although terrified of Mississippi itself, she signed up to participate in the Freedom Summer Project. Then her parents showed up and basically put her on house arrest.[2]

It didn't work, though.

Robinson had turned eighteen, so as much as they wanted to, her parents couldn't legally keep her from leaving. With the help of friends and movement leaders, money and a bus ticket were arranged. Her leaving played out into one of those all-too-familiar threats of "if you leave, don't ever return" situations. Robinson continued on, though, believing the fight against racial dehumanization was far more important.

She arrived in Laurel, Mississippi, with two others: Jimmy Garrett, a volunteer like herself, and Lester McKinney, the SNCC project director for the area. Laurel was seen as the most dangerous part of an already-dangerous state, so initially only three workers were being sent, and none of them white.[3]

After finally securing a place to stay, they had to find a place to work out of. While people appreciated what they were doing, no one who owned property would rent to them. Even those who owned empty buildings stated, "It's going to be destroyed if we rent to you." While they continued to search for suitable space, Robinson's worst fears came to pass: Lester McKinney was missing.[4]

McKinney's disappearance froze the blood not only of Robinson and Garrett, but also of those they reported it to. Unlike the majority of those entering Mississippi for the summer project, McKinney was a seasoned civil rights activist. Originally from Georgia, McKinney had organized and directed numerous protest activities and was one of the original Freedom Riders. For someone with his experience and political acumen to go missing could only mean the worst.

McKinney was also the fourth person the summer project had sent to be suddenly unaccounted for. Three people working in Meridian had been missing since June 21.[5]

Specific protocols were in place for this exact situation, and the Congress on Racial Equality had even printed out a security handbook to be given to all Mississippi workers and volunteers. In addition to directives about not traveling alone or at night, knowing when and where everyone was at all times was paramount. Anyone leaving their community center was required to phone in after arriving at their destination. "Should they be missing" the handbook stated, "project personnel will notify the Jackson office."[6]

This was exactly what happened in Meridian two weeks previously and was exactly what Robinson then did. She immediately alerted the Jackson office of COFO, as well as the SNCC office in Atlanta. This set off rapid-fire phone calls to the Justice Department and the FBI. Robinson also asked a group of local African American ministers for help, who agreed to make somewhat-covert inquiries with the Laurel police. All were hoping against hope to disprove the opinion of one journalist, who wrote, "A missing civil rights worker in Mississippi today is a dead civil rights worker."[7]

The news came from the FBI to the Jackson office: On the afternoon of July 7, McKinney had been arrested on an outstanding traffic ticket warrant. Held without bond or phone call, he had been transferred from the city jail to the work farm. His jailers had not fed him in over 48 hours.[8]

McKinney's arrest stemmed from the night before, when he went to help a sixteen-year-old named Terry Gillman, who was in a field, screaming and covered in blood. He and his younger brother had been attacked trying to enter the Burger Chef, a local diner. A group of white teens had blocked the entrance, asking them if they wanted to fight. When the two turned to leave, the large group of whites descended on the Gillmans, attacking them with long razors and bricks. They also chanted "Yankee go home" during the vicious beating, not realizing that their targets weren't civil rights workers from the north, but literally their neighbors.[9]

After getting both brothers to the hospital, McKinney called the police. His report was stalled because—knowing he had an outstanding warrant—he refused to give his name. He then returned to the café, finding what he fully expected to: a large group of African Americans had gathered outside the Burger Chef, armed with glass bottles. An even larger group of whites was marching down the street toward them. Police had fanned out in front of the restaurant. Rumors spread that the National Guard was on its way. Phone lines were cut.[10]

Miraculously, no more violence took place. Both groups dispersed at the urging of police. McKinney returned to the hospital and walked with the elder Gillman while carrying the younger home to his parents. The two boys were savagely beaten for trying to order a hamburger.

People had recognized McKinney, and his identity was soon made known to the police. He was arrested the following day.

PROJECT DIRECTOR

SNCC lawyers arrived to help McKinney just in time, as he was about to be sentenced to five years in Parchman Penitentiary. An agreement was reached in which all charges would be dropped on the condition that McKinney not return to Laurel for a period of five years.[11]

Ecstatic upon hearing McKinney was still alive, Robinson was less than happy with what came next: "SNCC asked me to become project director," she remembers. "And of course I wanted to die!" She told SNCC, "Are you kidding me? I know nothing about being a project director; that's not what I trained for!"[12]

"You had been involved in the student movement," the SNCC organizers told her, ignoring her objections. "You had gone to jail. You are from the South." And more importantly, "there is nobody but you." And eighteen-year-old Gwendolyn Robinson was promoted to project director in Laurel.[13]

Whatever apprehension she felt about leading the Laurel project, no one else felt that way about her. She had a "great ability to reach people," wrote John W. Herz, a forty-nine-year-old corporate attorney who spent two weeks in Laurel volunteering for the Lawyers' Civil Rights Program. "At first I underestimated her but I soon learned she had a rare ability to handle people and to reach Negro residents in the community."[14]

"She was dynamite," another volunteer recalled. "She ran that office"—not an easy thing to do. Robinson had to organize incoming and local volunteers, obtain permits, wrangle supplies, listen to death threats, and find a suitable location for the Freedom Library.[15]

This last task was also the most difficult: no one would rent to them. Carrie Clayton insisted they use her home, even though it was far too small and unsuitable (they did end up storing items on her porch). Eventually a wealthy real estate agent agreed to rent out a derelict building that had once been a dance hall for a ridiculously overpriced rent. Robinson was furious with him but relented, as there was simply no other choice. The community center was now being set up at Garden Oak Street, Laurel, Mississippi.

She wasn't the only one furious with the real estate shake-down. Whether they supported the Civil Rights Movement or not, numerous community members suddenly appeared to fix up the dilapidated dance hall, once known as Hee-Haws. New walls and windows were installed, the roof was repaired, and even the building's electrical system was restored. Not only was the owner charging the movement excessively, but he was also now getting a brand-new building out of it.[16]

LAUREL FREEDOM LIBRARY

In no more than a week or two, Robinson and her help transformed Hee-Haws into a workable office, a large hall for meetings and classes, and a library. Robinson remembers the library as being "one of our crowning achievements." It would be vital to their work in Laurel.[17]

"Black people have never been able to use the public library and often their school libraries were very small. In their public schools, the books were so precious they wouldn't let them take them home." But now they could. "People from around the country had sent books and boxes and boxes of books." Slightly more than 1,500 volumes were now available for checkout at Laurel's Freedom Library.[18]

Use was tentative at first, but soon more and more children of all ages were making good use of the library. Then the adults came. This was astounding. The bravery needed to overcome the severest and most acute library anxiety, which went well beyond feelings of shame and inadequacy, remains phenomenal. "For many adults," Robinson recalls, "it was their first time ever in a library." A lifelong fear of real-world consequences more than shame had to be overcome just to walk through the door. It must have been the most amazing experience to witness.[19]

The Freedom Libraries had a habit of making the amazing seem commonplace. Robinson was an expert at highlighting such experiences. "In some cases," she stated, "the parents are illiterate. And the children would read them stories," a reversal of typical library story times. Those assigned to teaching in the classroom had to revise their curriculum to include beginning literacy classes for adults. This "was very, very important to have as a resource; as part of the social justice movement."[20]

No list survives of exactly what books were available to the residents of Laurel, but a want list was circulated out of the Hattiesburg Freedom Library by its director, Sanford Leigh, and is indicative of what Freedom Libraries had, and what was needed. "Books by and about Negroes" was first on their list. Authors wanted included Ralph Ellison, Richard Wright, Countee Cullen, and James Baldwin. They did not want Baldwin's *Go Tell It on the Mountain*, but they did need many more copies of James Silver's *The Closed Society* and *Stride toward Freedom* by Martin Luther King Jr.

Basic vocabulary children's books were in high need as well, with a special request for "integrated story books and stories in which Negro children are the protagonists, also Negro history for children." For those interested in more comprehensive lists, both the New York and Chicago public libraries had relevant lists ready for anyone who asked. Hattiesburg was also in need of books and pamphlets about the Civil Rights Movement itself and works about nonviolence. Also listed were various addresses of organizations who published and collected this type of item.

Those who wished to help were urged to send either money or books, but "since we may not have a full-time librarian to order books, it is better to send books than money." It would also be helpful if pamphlets could be arranged in a binder, which could then be circulated immediately. Of course, no library in history would ever turn away monetary donations. "If you do send money," Leigh closed his want list with, "send postal money orders made out to Sanford Leigh and indicate that the money is to be used for the library."[21]

Leigh also had another issue taking up his time: Robinson would not stop calling him.

Although one of the strongest leaders the organizers of Freedom Summer could have ever hoped for (one of "the baddest, baddest, baddest organizers in the SNCC"), Robinson could not do it all. Besides organizing volunteers and locals, teaching herself to drive,

Although the Hattiesburg Freedom Library has a large number of books, there
are many glaring gaps in our collection. You can help to fill in these gaps.

1. Books by and about Negroes: Negro history; fiction - Richard Wright, James
Baldwin (we don't need Go Tell It on the Mountain), Ralph Ellison, some of the
lesser known modern writers; poetry - Countee Cullen, Langston Hughes, Gwendolyn Brooks; books about the nature of prejudice; anything dealing with the
situation of Negroes in this country. We need many, many more copies of The
Closed Society by James Silver and Stride Toward Freedom by Martin Luther King, Jr.

2. Books for children, especially books with very simple vocabularies. We
very badly need "integrated" story books and stories in which Negro children
are the protagonists, also Negro history for children.

You can obtain titles of the books suggested above from a number of organizations.
For instance, I have such a list, prepared by the NAACP of Oxford, Ohio:
"Books for Inter-racial Understanding." Other lists are:
    "Books About Negro Life for Children" -- The New York Public Library
    "Books for Friendship" (children's books), 50¢ - American Friends Service
        Committee, 160 N. 15th St., Philadelphia 2, Pa.
    "On These We Stand" -- Chicago Public Library
    "Books for Brotherhood" -- National Conference of Christians and Jews,
        43 West 57th St., New York 19, NY.

Sandie Leigh's "Want List" for the Hattiesburg Freedom Library. *Courtesy
of Wisconsin State Historical Society.*

instituting dress and dating codes, and not flinching when law enforcement pointed guns at her, she desperately needed someone to
run the library for her.[22]

WATS line reports, transcripts of wide area telephone service,
record Robinson making numerous pleas with Leigh in Hattiesburg. Someone named Sheila there was running the Hattiesburg
Freedom Library but wanted to go to Laurel as much as Robinson
wanted her there. She placed numerous calls, but her Hattiesburg
counterpart would not let Sheila go until he found a replacement
for her.

Frustrated, Robinson made plans to simply drive to Hattiesburg
herself and bring Sheila back with her. Before she could, Leigh
called her, stating he had put Sheila on a bus and sent her home.
According to the WATS line report, Sheila's boyfriend had shown
up to party with some friends, and "there was an orgie (sic) of sorts

held in local houses of whom the parent was away." Leigh rightfully felt this behavior would do nothing but damage the entire project; he was sending others back home as well, mostly for their inability to take direction or be part of a team.[23]

While both directors struggled through July, the town of Greenville got lucky. The Freedom Library there was getting an actual and professionally trained librarian.

Sort of.

CHILDREN LISTENING TO DR. SEUSS

Virginia Steele is the name most associated with Freedom Libraries. She did more to organize, streamline, and project a semblance of shared practices to the project. Yet like Gwen Robinson, she too "wanted to die" when positions of responsibility were suddenly thrust on her.[24]

After years of teaching elementary school, Steele enrolled in UCLA's School of Librarianship. In the spring of 1964, and only a few months before graduating, she met a group of African American students at Stanford University who were discussing the upcoming Freedom Summer project. "They spoke with enthusiasm and inspiration about books and ways to get them into people's hands," she recalled. Steele was clearly interested in what they were saying, but what they told her next was amazing: their experience of "children listening to a Dr. Seuss story when they had never heard anything like that" may have been the catalyst that caused Steele to join the summer project. It was certainly something that would cause the eyes of those who heard about it to well up. That deceptively simple sentence almost sums up the entire purpose of Freedom Libraries, not to mention the Civil Rights Movement. It would take a hardened heart not to be moved by it.[25]

Steele contacted the organizers of Freedom Summer and expressed her willingness to help out. If they were in need of any professional library assistance, "I am sure I can get some pretty good help from the teachers here at the library school." She heard from them a few weeks later, but it wasn't a thank-you note. "We were very glad to find that a professional librarian is joining the Mississippi Summer Project. We would like to ask you to be in charge of one of these Freedom Libraries for the summer." As she read in disbelief, the letter's *P.S.* drove the message home: "Bring some 3×5 cards with you."[26]

Having not yet graduated and having never worked in a library, Steele found herself committing to the project. That her last final exam was on the history of printing and not setting up a library only seemed to reinforce her apprehension in taking on such a role, but she soon found herself driving to Oxford, Ohio. After the administrators at Kentucky's Berea College backed out at the last minute, Oxford's Western College for Women welcomed all Freedom Summer participants for their week of condensed training. Being asked to coordinate all the Freedom Libraries and their volunteers appeared to Steele at the time to be "a blind piece of planning," but it turned out not to be. Besides her years of teaching, being older than most, and having a newly minted library degree, she also had one characteristic that was more important than anything on her resume: Steele's "capacity for hope" stood out above all other achievements. A year later she would agree that this aspect of her personality had been the most important.[27]

She gave her cadre of volunteers a crash course in basic librarianship, and together they made book pockets and checkout cards out of envelopes and the 3×5 cards she had brought. She recommended books on cataloging, storytelling, and book repair. What was most important was the ability to issue library cards, a critical tool in building a user's self-worth.[28]

Emotional highs and lows marked almost everyone's experience in Oxford, and Steele was no different. An impromptu field trip to Oxford's public library gave her much-needed inspiration, while nonviolent training was distressing for her. "Imagine how I felt," she wrote to friends back home. "While I was learning how to drop on the ground to protect my face, my ears, and my breasts, I was asked to coordinate all the libraries in the entire project. I wanted to cry."[29]

Steele arrived in Greenville, Mississippi, in early June. The site for the library was an apartment located above a beauty salon and

900 block of Nelson Street, Greenville, Mississippi, 1964. The Freedom Library was located behind the two vehicles on the right. *Courtesy of the Nelken Archives/Greenville History Museum.*

shoe repair store. She had no sooner arrived than she was startled by a huge bang. The books had arrived, all twenty thousand of them.

GREENVILLE FREEDOM LIBRARY

The books were supposed to get there ahead of her, but the delivery truck's tires had been repeatedly slashed. Also, one of the trucks had been seized and the driver arrested on a phony charge of transporting stolen goods. The drivers were understandably terrified and emptied the boxes onto the street before speeding away. But a human chain soon formed, and people of all ages—including a local drunk who could barely stand—helped get the books into the new library.[30]

Besides this act of community benevolence, Steele found it very hard to be there. The heat was unbearable, and someone had walked off with her wallet. Disputing the phrase "we are not afraid"—taken from the lyrics of Pete Seeger's updated version of "We Shall Overcome"—Steele had no misgivings in reporting that "we *were* afraid." While she and her volunteers were busy trying to organize a functioning library, hostile whites surrounded the building, driving around and following workers.[31]

Fear also manifested itself for Steele with her assumption of being watched from within. "In Greenville the Freedom School and Library is located on Broadway," states a Mississippi State Sovereignty Commission report dated August 15, 1964. Although the state already had the Ku Klux Klan and the White Citizens' Council, it somehow felt it needed one more agency to protect itself against the *Brown v. Board of Education* ruling and all that went with it. With a mission to "do and perform any and all acts and things deemed necessary and proper to protect the sovereignty of the state of Mississippi," the commission "channeled tax dollars to the Citizens Council, hired informants, organized mass mailings and . . . turned over information on subversives to the FBI."[32]

"The purpose of this trip was meet with Virginia Steele," the August 15 report continued, "a white female from Ohio who is about 35 to 40 years old. She is a volunteer worker in Greenville and is connected with the Library Program."[33]

Besides intimidation, what good this type of reporting did is anyone's guess. Steele also faced other difficulties, including watching a COFO worker burn a stack of donated *Reader's Digest*s who was vehemently opposed to the political slant of the magazine.[34]

The culmination of all this left Steele disheartened. "I have been so depressed about the library I couldn't bear to face it," she wrote a friend. She was able to push on, though, and even received help from the unlikeliest of people: Lura Currier.[35]

Steele had reached out to the Mississippi Library Commission and the American Library Association for assistance just prior to arriving in Greenville. While the ALA responded to her request by providing advice and pamphlets on "simple circulation routines," she received no response from the MLC. Yet for reasons still not clear, Steele had a prolonged and helpful telephone conversation with Currier on July 25.[36]

The two discussed Currier's frustration with the ALA, and—long before high-interest low-vocabulary books existed—her attempts to get publishers to print such books. Steele would later state that Currier was "very sympathetic to the Freedom Libraries," but surviving evidence doesn't really support this. Currier was not at all happy with John Fischer's editorial in *Harper's* asking readers to donate books to the Freedom Summer project. Nor was she pleased with money and supplies being given to libraries not under her purview.

In a letter dated August 4, Currier explains to Steele that the reason African Americans didn't have access to libraries in Mississippi was because "we did not have library service for ANYBODY in most of the state." Steele appears to have missed or chose to ignore the not-so-subtle subtext of this line of reasoning (why should black people have libraries when white people don't?).[37]

Steele understood what Currier never appeared to: "Negroes at this time need to see books by and about Negroes, their life, problems, history, art, [and] contribution." With the help of the summer project volunteers, at least one spy, and "courageous local residents who appeared at her door to shelve as well as borrow books," the Greenville Freedom Library was quickly able to open its doors.[38]

It must have been an amazing sight. Shelves bursting with approximately ten thousand books carefully arranged by subject, with classification letters drawn onto each one's spine. Of course, all this order went out the window, as well as the traditional method of checking out books. Abandoning what she called her "cataloguing phantasy," Steele, like any good librarian, gave herself over to the needs of her patrons.[39]

One of her first actions under this new attitude was to no longer classify easy-to-read children's books as such. "Adults or young people who are unable to read more difficult things are extremely shy about reaching for them." Shelving them among the books for adults was critical in reducing the painful and humiliating shame felt by those with little or no literacy.[40]

The denial of basic literacy and library services had made the now open collection a novelty to the citizens of Greenville. The books themselves were treated like a new pet, brought home and shown off. The more time that passed, the more family members became used to its presence. People simply had no experience with taking a book home. Steele would remind other library workers of this crucial point, making sure they understood the "opportunities we have with this mass of books and these people who had had almost no opportunity or time or encouragement to become familiar with books and their worth." Teens especially "got a kick out of a school book out of school."[41]

Besides running her own library, Steele had also been in charge of coordinating the other Freedom Libraries in Mississippi—not an easy thing and somewhat of a logistical nightmare. She did, however, make road trips to other cities—her Volkswagen bus dubbed "The Freedom Bus"—and assisted in answering questions, delivering books, and driving people to and from voter registration drives.

"And then," she wrote a year later for the *California Librarian*, "I did library work." This would include preparing "source material for classes, set up an open file of magazines with articles of particular interest, and devised a technique for having them open directly to the article, made bulletin boards and kept them up, instituted library crafts activities with the children and held story hour for them."[42]

Fifty miles east in the town of Greenwood, a story hour had gone horribly wrong. Lorna Smith—a seventy-year-old, blue-haired grandmother from California—was reading to a group of children outside in the city park. As more and more children gathered to listen to her, Smith could hear someone screaming racial epithets at her. It was the police.

Instead of ignoring them, Smith stopped reading and calmly walked over to the policemen who were yelling at her from their cruiser. She offered them her outstretched hand and asked the two to join her in reading to the kids. Recognizing she was not a Greenwood local, they told her to go back home and to "stop fool'n' with niggers."[43]

At this point a concerned woman came to assist Smith, but one of the policemen shouted, "Get out of here you black bitch, we don't need you here!"

"Can't we be friends?" Smith asked in all sincerity. "I have a son just about your age." The police drove off, leaving Smith to console the brave woman who tried to help her.[44]

Smith was a rarity among the volunteers that summer. This fearless senior citizen had served as a nurse in the First World War, and had been a research assistant to both Upton Sinclair and Theodore Dreiser. She had traveled the world, raised a family, and had lived a "rich, full life." And then in the spring of 1964 she learned about the call for volunteers in Mississippi for the upcoming summer. "I saw on television that they wanted people," she stated. So she went.[45]

GREENWOOD FREEDOM LIBRARY

She bypassed the required training in Oxford and arrived in Greenwood in mid-June. Her first job—after securing lodging with a local family—was to try and organize what was supposed to be Greenwood's Freedom Library. Whatever the original intentions had been (see chapter 1), the upstairs rooms at 708 Avenue N had become nothing but a rat-infested dumping ground.

Smith felt it looked how "Hitler's pile for bonfires looked, boxed books, boxes broken open, books falling out, books unboxed." She spent five or six hours each morning cleaning and organizing, by which time she would go change clothes and then walk to the city park to read to the groups of children who had gathered there. After reading, she would pass out donated children's books, Sunday school pamphlets, and magazines for the children to color. She would then spend her evenings canvassing Greenwood, encouraging and offering to help people to register to vote.[46]

"Children came all day for beaten up books," she recalled. Both children and adults made frequent requests for Bibles they could keep. Not having any, Smith wrote to the American Bible Society for donations. Smith continued this routine for most of June, happy to see returning faces to her afternoon story times. A young girl dragged her baby brother to the park daily, pretending it was all her sibling's idea: "He said you said for him to come again today."[47]

Before June was even over, two lifelong friendships were made with Smith. One was with Stokely Carmichael—one of the most courageous and dedicated (and later controversial) figures of the entire Civil Rights Movement. Beginning with the Freedom Rides, Carmichael "had his hands in every major civil rights demonstration and event." A charismatic and natural leader, Carmichael appeared in Freedom Libraries all over Mississippi as well as in Alabama and Arkansas (see chapters 5 and 7), greeting and instructing the wide-eyed volunteers from the North of what to expect.[48]

It is not exactly clear who was enamored more with whom. Smith felt Carmichael was "destined for greatness," while Carmichael was frequently bent over in "bouts of hysterics" over a story Smith was telling him. They would visit and write each other long after Freedom Summer, well into Carmichael's split from the Civil Rights Movement.[49]

The other lifelong friend of Smith's was someone she had already known. Sally Belfrage arrived at the end of June in Greenwood to continue running the library Smith had prepared. After encountering each other in the home of Smith's host family, Belfrage extended her hand to her. Smith's remembrance of the meeting is worth quoting in full:

> "I'm Sally," the young woman informed me, I stood, my old mind not functioning as quickly as it once did. "Sally Belfrage," she added. Grabbing her in my arms, I invited her to sleep with me, without even consulting my hostess. Daughter of my friend, Cedric Belfrage, I first saw Sally when a babe of six weeks. I last saw her in London in 1957. Her father's book, "South of God," came out in 1941. In my copy is penned, "My deep respect and affection as always to Lorna who stays on the north side-west anyway. Cedrick Belfrage, Hollywood, March 13th, 1941."[50]

As the world shrunk that day in the town of Greenwood, Smith was simply overjoyed. "With such good hands as Sally's in which to leave the library, I felt no guilty conscience in returning home."[51]

It is unknown if Lorna Smith had a bigger impact on Greenwood, or if Greenwood had a bigger impact on Smith. The head of her host family would write, "We miss you very much and what hurt me so is that we may never see you again." Smith, back home in California, watching the continuing onslaught of racial violence and hate continue to play out across her television, would sit back and "turn my thoughts to the little Negro children I read to daily on the playgrounds, their numbers increasing daily. Clustered around

Sally Belfrage, Mississippi, 1964. *Courtesy of Eve Pomerance (Sally's daughter).*

me, they were the personification of love and appreciation, eager and begging for more."[52]

What the children begged for would now come from Sally Belfrage. Younger, taller, and much blonder than the matronly Smith, Belfrage had arrived in Greenwood for a different reason: her heart was broken.

CALIFORNIA RADICAL

Belfrage was also from California, being raised there by her British parents, both of whom were prominent yet radical authors, and both of whom were jailed and deported for their un-American activities during the McCarthy era. Belfrage herself wrote numerous

Page from Sally Belfrage's diary, dated June 1964. *Courtesy of Eve Pomerance.*

books, including *A Room in Moscow* which was published not long before she volunteered for the summer project.

Like Virginia Steele, she too had to attend the weeklong training session at Oxford's Western College for Women. Besides the uncomfortable, humiliating, and nonviolent training, Belfrage took in lectures from Stokely Carmichael, John Doar, and Vincent Harding. She also heard Bob Moses ask if anyone had read *The Fellowship of the Ring* by J. R. R. Tolkien. "There is a weariness," Moses stated, "from constant attention to the things you are doing, the struggle of good against evil." (As this quote does not appear in Tolkien's work, it remains unknown if Moses misquoted Tolkien, or Belfrage misquoted Moses.)[53]

As the buses left Ohio for Mississippi, many volunteers offered either false or real bravado, dismissing tales of terror and violence with "this is still America" statements. After what happened to her parents, though, Belfrage knew better. Writing of her father thirty years later, she would state, "Perhaps he was most pleased about my going to Mississippi in 1964 to work in the civil rights movement," as well as her motive for going. "I had a broken heart and was interested in ending it all. My sacrifice to a lynch mob, I thought, wouldn't hurt him too much."[54]

All of this changed with her arrival in Greenwood, from the love and affection shown to her by her host family, the brief reuniting with Lorna Smith, and her experience in running the Freedom Library.

By the time she inherited it, the Greenwood Freedom Library was the busiest one in all of Mississippi. "The library," Belfrage wrote, "my future domain, spread over most of the second floor—a large, light, square room with windows on three sides, divided by waist-high partitions. . . . Books spilled off shelves, out of boxes, and around the floor." She could not determine whether there were more books or people in the library. It was full of civil rights workers, some sleeping, some talking, one person playing a guitar under a sign that said "no guitar playing." In addition to the volunteers, the place was packed with local people, and "children of all sizes ran among prone bodies, trunks, bags, boxes, books, and knots of the newly arrived." Carmichael was there, admonishing the newly arrived about observing local customs, when and where it was safe to travel, and to "never leave a jail at night."[55]

Belfrage spent her days following a similar routine. After washing the breakfast dishes at her host family's place (which they protested, refusing to believe when she told them she had washed dishes all her life), she would open up the doors to the library. This was more of a pretense, as the doors were typically unlocked anyway, with more and more volunteers crashing there during the night.

Lorna Smith had created a cataloging system, but it appeared to be of little help, so Belfrage disregarded it. She found the shelves marked "fiction" to be overflowing with "scores of Horatio Algers, nineteenth-century ladies' books, some valuable-looking first editions, numbered sets of Thackeray, Dickens, and Conan Doyle, eleven copies of *The Vicar of Wakefield*." She then settled into a routine of actual library work, unloading boxes of books onto the shelves, "adding, discarding, arranging." Most of the donated boxes were questionable—such as the survey of British fiction—but occasionally something great would show up, such as "a useful carton of new children's picture books; American, Southern, or Negro histories; how-to books—good things."[56]

Soon, Justice Department lawyers and out-of-state reporters began to hang out at the library as well, making the crowded place all the more crowded, causing Belfrage to work and weave around even more bodies. Besides checking in and out books, Belfrage also manned the library's one phone line, which was mainly used to harass her. Callers wanted to know if she was a real blonde, about her sexual relations with African Americans, and whether or not she valued her life.[57]

"Dear Sally, How are you doing as a librarian. The first time I saw you, I start thinking, she smiled at me it best for me to start smiling back." So opened a letter Belfrage received from Lucius Murphy—a local thirteen-year-old with a very big crush on her. "I wish I could work in the libarie with you, do the thing libarian should do."[58]

Belfrage also assisted in voter-registration activities and literacy classes, the former causing her to spend a few nights in jail. She also noted that it wasn't just the segregated library that prevented citizens from free access to information. The town had no bookstore, but books were for sale at Fisher Stationery. Their selection was dismal, however, consisting of Civil War histories, cookbooks, and religious items. Belfrage noted that everyday publications outside of the state were smuggled in, such as James Silver's *Mississippi: The Closed Society* and the *Saturday Evening Post*. Radio and television were also heavily censored by the state, and the Ku Klux Klan had been showering Greenwood with flyers dropped from an airplane. This may explain why the Freedom Library was always so busy. Like all good libraries, it had become the hub of the community.[59]

Like Smith before her, Belfrage tried to make connections with all who crossed her path. While trying to help bail out a local volunteer, she asked law enforcement officers if they knew where William Faulkner had lived. This appeared to erase what she called "white Greenwood outrage," as everyone had a friend of a friend of a friend who knew him. Stories about Faulkner's antics were abundant, although no one seemed to know where he had lived or read one of his books to completion.[60]

Her greatest connection was with her host family. Her daily interactions with them were telling: she exasperated herself trying to get them to sit down with her while she ate, to stop calling her "Miss Sally," and that it was perfectly okay for the teenage son to look at her. Except it wasn't okay for the teen to look at her—that was how her host family had raised him. "Jus' one boy touch a white girl's hand," the mother told Belfrage. "He be in the river in two hours."[61]

She also wanted Belfrage to know that African Americans didn't have offensive hygiene, as was written in the flyers the Klan had dropped from above. "Everybody stink if they don't have a bath," she said, clearly worried about Belfrage's opinion of her. "Everybody got a odor. Even a cat got a odor."[62]

Belfrage left Greenwood in the last week of August, which was the problem of Freedom Summer—it was only one summer. Arriving home, she found a letter from her young admirer waiting for her. "When they say you was gone I start criing. I said Why! Why! Why! Didn't someone tell me she was going to leave. . . . I am not going to forget that great American Sally Belfrage."[63]

Before she left, Belfrage was able to help facilitate *In White America*—a play by Martin Duberman—and put on by the Free Southern Theater. Very few residents of Greenwood had ever seen a play before, and even those who had had never seen anything quite like this before. This was an interactive performance, with the audience engaging in dialogue with the actors. In her diary of the summer, Belfrage wrote, "It was the most exciting theater I had ever seen; it was about the people for whom it was performed."[64]

The Free Southern Theater was born in the winter of 1963, created by two SNCC field directors and a newspaper reporter. Having met at a drama workshop at Tougaloo College in Jackson, Mississippi, and with the help of Richard Schechner from Tulane University, they created a document titled *A General Prospectus for the Establishment of a Free Southern Theater*. Proposing to "estab-

Free Southern Theater performance of *In White America*, McComb, Mississippi, 1964. *Courtesy of Shirley Martin Bates.*

lish a legitimate theater in the deep south," the four hoped "to bring in artists from outside the state as well as to provide the opportunity for local people with creative ability to have experience with the theater," as well as "emphasise the universality of the problems of the Negro people."[65]

FINE ARTS IN McCOMB

The Free Southern Theater visited a handful of Freedom Libraries and Schools in Mississippi during Freedom Summer. Members of the theater didn't just perform and leave. They stayed with volunteer host families or other local residents, assisted in voter registration, and helped out in the Community Centers.

One person enamored with the performers was McComb's Shirley Martin. A daily visitor to the McComb Freedom School, Martin was given something she had wanted her entire life: an art lesson. The simple act of being shown how to paint was something denied to McComb's African Americans. Free Southern Theater performer Denise Nicholas gave Martin some instruction on watercolor paint techniques. It changed Martin's life.

"We would come straight after school and go directly to the Freedom School and sit under the tree for lessons," Martin remembers. "I was interested in art. They didn't have it in our schools, they only had it in regular [white] schools. Denise Nicholas would teach me art, and after a bit, I got pretty good at it." Which is a bit of understatement. Martin would win three regional art awards and earn a scholarship to a New York art school. Unfortunately, still being a minor, her parents wouldn't allow her to attend. "My mother said no because I was a girl and we can't go away from home ever."[66]

Martin started protesting for her civil rights when she was only ten years old. That was when a handful of students from Burglund High School tried to order lunch from the Woolworth's cafeteria on McComb's main street. They were quickly arrested. "Only whites were supposed to eat there," Martin said. "That's why they went to jail, because they were eating there."[67]

When the students returned to school from jail, they were expelled. More than one hundred students then walked out in protest, demanding that their fellow students be reinstated. Martin was part of this second group, and as young as she was, she too was arrested and spent three nights in jail. Upon her return to school, the authorities insisted that she and her fellow students who participated in the walkout sign a pledge never to take part in civil rights activities (as well as endure a 10 percent drop in their current grades). Martin refused to sign. Her uncompromising bravery sparked a second student walkout. "It was worth it," she recalls. "I would do it all over again."[68]

Shirley Martin Bates to-
day, holding a photo of
herself from 1961 when
she first became involved
in the Civil Rights Move-
ment. *Photo by Tully
Taylor. Courtesy of Tully
Taylor.*

It was this part of daily life in McComb that made the Freedom
School and its library of such a high importance in Martin's life
and those of others like her. Located at 702 Wall Street, Freedom
House (as it was called) was actually three structures owned by
Hilary Cotton and Antoine McNulty—both eager supporters of
the summer project. Much like Greenwood, McComb's Freedom

Shirley Martin's older brother Joe at the McComb Freedom Library. *Courtesy of Shirley Martin Bates.*

House was a hive of activity, acting as a school, a library, and a place for the out-of-state volunteers to sleep.[69]

"I can set up a library along with the new freedom school and the children would have their own place, wouldn't have to worry about going to that other library where nobody wants them touching anything. I can just see it." So said Michigan college student Celeste Tyree, in Denise Nicholas's 2005 novel *Freshwater Road*, labeled "the best work of fiction about the civil rights movements"

Civil rights worker Dory Ladner outside the back of the McComb Freedom School. *Courtesy of Shirley Martin Bates.*

by numerous publications. Nicholas's time spent in McComb and other cities while she toured with the Free Southern Theater influenced much of this work.[70]

She was extremely flattered that Martin remembers her giving a few brief art lessons more than half a century later. "I did have a healthy interest in visual arts," she recalls. "I took Art History classes at University of Michigan before joining Free Southern Theater." Impressed by the libraries she visited over the summer, Nicholas and other members of the Free Southern Theater would set up a Freedom Library the following year in the 9th Ward of New Orleans (see chapter 7). "Our space functioned as a mini community center with performance space, library, and offices. I loved that space as children began to buzz in and out, curious, hungry for learning and full of energy."[71]

This buzzing was exactly the kind of activity going on at 702 Wall Street in McComb that summer.

And then it was bombed.

Chapter Four

—————————◯—————————

White Backlash
35 Shootings, 80 Beatings, 65 Bombings

"THE PAIN GROWS WORSE with each bombing."[1]

It was the morning of July 8, 1964, when the McComb Freedom House was bombed. A bundle of dynamite had been placed just outside an open window, exploding with a fierce roar that shook the entire city. Curtis Hayes—one of ten people sleeping inside the Freedom House at the time—was severely lacerated by shards of window glass. "I don't recall hearing any noise," he would later testify. "I only remember lying on the floor beside my bed under glass from the window and the lumber from the window frame. . . . When I finally made it to safety (the kitchen) I was still quite dazed and noticed that I was bleeding profusely. I later learned that my body was covered with small cuts, and some 30 of them were deep cuts."[2]

Not far from Hayes was co-worker Dennis Sweeney, who received a concussion from the blast. Unbelievably, the remaining eight workers survived with no injuries. Residents of McComb rushed to the scene to offer help, many of them carrying guns, abandoning the creed of nonviolence (at least for this morning). When the police finally arrived, one officer opined, "It must have been termites."[3]

Amid the books, the story times, the plays, and all the hope the Freedom Libraries brought with them, it is sometimes easy to forget that at the time, Mississippi "was a region seething with hatred,

53

where there appeared to be no restraints against white violence."[4] Bombings—a favorite tactic of the Ku Klux Klan—would continue to rock McComb all summer.

None of it worked, though.

McComb's Freedom House turned out not to be the building itself. As soon as school was let out that day, the children rushed to 702 Wall Street and simply sat outside waiting for the teachers and library workers to tend to them. Shirley Martin remembers sitting under a tree while teachers "taught us history and math. I was interested in art and law, which they taught to us too. I was always wanted to learn what our laws were." Life skills were also taught in addition to academics. "We sit out on the ground and talk about things that we need to know about hygiene or whatever. Whatever we need to know they taught us."[5]

Free access to books was also paramount for McComb African Americans. "We had all kinds of books in the library that we can go check out if we wanted to," Martin recalls, noting the amazement this unheard-of practice brought. "We had it tough back then. But I remember checking out books. Books!"[6]

The scorching July heat meant that outdoor classes could not go on much longer, and with whatever could be salvaged from the smouldering remains, the McComb Freedom House reopened in a church basement not far from the original location. Although the city continued to be "under a state of siege," children and adults continued to utilize both the library and the volunteer teachers, and even managed to publish a school newsletter. McComb's *Freedom's Journal*, named after the very first African American newspaper, was full of local news, interviews, original poems, book reviews, and some truly horrible jokes from the youngest children.[7]

"Isn't it awful not to be able to go to / a public library and get an interesting book / without being put out and given / a hateful look."[8] As one can see by this excerpt of the poem *Isn't It Awful* by Edith Moore, free access to libraries remained a high priority for McComb's youth. White violence was not going to stop them.

White violence would not stop the Freedom Library in Meridian either, located 170 miles northeast of McComb. As mentioned earlier (chapter 2), the Meridian Freedom Library began months before the summer project began and was run by the husband-and-wife team of Mickey and Rita Schwerner.

Oddly enough, the Schwerners almost didn't come to Mississippi at all, as their initial application to work for the SNCC was rejected. Months before the northern invasion of primarily white students from the North, civil and voting rights organizations were cautious about sending white people for various reasons, not the least being the amount of time it would take for southern communities to trust outsiders. Although both were highly recommended, "SNCC chose a Negro couple over them."[9]

MERIDIAN COMMUNITY CENTER

The SNCC was not the only organization, though, and the Schwerners were accepted by CORE. After saying goodbye to friends and family, giving notice at their jobs (Rita was an English teacher and Mickey a social worker), subletting their apartment, and giving away their dog Gandhi, the two arrived in Meridian on the evening of January 19, 1964. Five spacious and empty second-story rooms awaited them at 2505 5th Street, in a building owned by a local pharmacist. The decrepit, filthy, and probably unsafe structure did not dampen the couple's enthusiasm in any way. "We didn't notice the cold, the dirt, the decay, or the emptiness," Rita told a reporter. "We only saw the rooms as we hoped to make them: colorful, filled with books, and the sounds of music and happy people."[10]

"Filled with books" would end up being an understatement, as thousands of them had been sent from Tougaloo College, the city of Jackson, Mississippi, and New York. With donated money the two were able to purchase lumber and paint. Most of January was spent organizing a working office and cataloging the books as each new crate arrived. Mickey helped some local teens—David and Marshall Sims and James Chaney—build a ping pong table in one of the empty rooms, which would function as a teen room.[11]

Using a donated mimeo machine, flyers were printed on the back of discarded letterhead from Pittsburgh's Alcoa Aluminum. The Schwerners handed out the flyers on the street, but also at one of T. J. Harris High School's basketball games. Initially Mickey was told to "get off the campus and not come back" by the school's principal, but he and Rita attended the game anyway, cheering on the home team while handing out flyers.[12]

This leaflet promoted "The Meridian Community Center," its address, and that anyone and everyone was welcome, seven days a week. The center offered "a library with 10,000 books, many of which you can't get elsewhere." More importantly, "You may take books out free." Also advertised was homework help, story times, and even sewing classes.[13]

While alerting the community that a story hour would take place every Saturday at 2:00 p.m., the flyer emphasized the important fact that "young children are also allowed to take books home at no cost." Rita would also institute a "no fine" policy, believing "that if children especially have overdue books, we do not want to discourage their coming to the center by having a fine due." She also made the critical observation that "some people, too, have never owned a book and if they want a book that badly (not that many of course) it is felt that it would help them more than it would hurt the library."[14]

Rita would make all kinds of ingenious and humane statements like this throughout her and her husband's stay in Mississippi. She appeared to have a genuine predisposition for librarianship, conducting mental needs assessments and filling them as quickly as the available resources would allow. Her story times were not just reading a book to interested children. She arranged for transportation for those who needed it, provided snacks and drinks, sang songs, and let the children take turns reading as well. She also let the children explore the library, a novel and foreign experience for them. "I usually let the children wander until they feel at home," Rita remarked, noting how they "delighted in the freedom they were given to wander around the library and take out books without rush."[15]

Daily homework help was also available, with Rita creating arithmetic flash cards and vocabulary word games for the older children who showed up after regular school. As the weeks went by, she realized none of the teen girls or women she encountered

Rita Schwerner and David Halberstam at the summer project orientation, Oxford, Ohio. *Photo by Galen Gockel. Courtesy of Galen Gockel.*

had ever owned a new dress. Rita immediately sought donations of a sewing machine from a friend and material from a garment manufacturer, both in New York. By April, Rita was able to report, "Some 125 women are now sewing at home, with about 25 more women and girls receiving instruction daily." Noticing that the sewing program was bringing both the rural poor and the middle class, Rita was happy to report, "I believe we have found one of the programs which we were searching for—an entrance into the Negro community."[16]

Mickey had made inroads into the community as well, beginning with a class he held for high school dropouts. Soon the teens began to check out books from the library, returning frequently to see what new arrivals the library received, as well as requesting "well known" books that they hoped the library would be able to fulfill. A donated phonograph, records, and a film projector were also available for use, although actual films were unavailable due to lack of funds.[17]

Mickey's own needs assessment of the community saw him holding more evening classes, including how to properly fill out applications for retail store positions and civil service jobs, both closed to African Americans. He spent his days venturing into the heart of Meridian neighborhoods (usually with James Chaney as his guide), engaging in voter-registration work and letting others know what the community center had to offer. Mickey was also in charge of facility and financial logistics, including organizing and sorting donations, managing budgets and volunteers, and writing reports.[18]

The library had no formal classification system, but was divided among subjects such as "poetry, drama, essays, fiction, juvenile

All about Us by Eva Knox Evans. *Photo by author.*

books, race relations, [and] sociology." While no complete list survives (and probably was never made), Meridian did have "1000 copies of David Copperfield, several hundred copies of a science book, and about 100 copies of a folk song anthology." The library also had "several more James Baldwin books, which are extremely popular."[19]

It was, however, Eva Knox Evans's *All about Us* that made a remarkable impact. Rita read it for her Saturday story time on April 11. "We talked about it and related the story to Meridian," she noted, "talking especially about the separate schools and why they might exist." Then came an observation that not only summed up the entire Civil Rights Movement but could also solve modern-day race relations: "The answers came from the children." After discussing the book a bit further, "The children then drew pictures of people of various colors working together."[20]

MISSISSIPPI'S BEST HOPE

"Yesterday the police picked up Mickey," Rita noted in a report. Although they had not been heavily bothered or harassed since their arrival, the closer things got to the summer project, the more pushback those involved with the community center began to feel.

When Mickey was attempting to purchase some of the books the teens had requested, a policeman arrested him at the department store's book counter and took him to the police station. Mickey was interviewed for a few minutes, then released with no charges. This type of harassment continued, and Mickey was once again arrested in early May, this time charged with "blocking a crosswalk."[21]

Although the pushback in Meridian was growing, and half of the community was "severely frightened," the Schwerners continued their work. In one of his final reports, Mickey wrote, "The library is functioning very well with many books in circulation." He then concluded, "One of the most important functions of the center we have found is that it serves as a place where people can come for whatever purpose they want."[22]

Both Schwerners left Meridian in June to help out with the orientation and training of the summer movement volunteers in Ohio.

Here they intersected with many of the people featured in this book, including Bob Moses, Dave Dennis, Virginia Steele, Gwen Robinson, and Sally Belfrage. On June 20 Mickey drove a packed station wagon back to Meridian, showing the summer volunteers the community center and helping them secure accommodation. Rita stayed behind in Ohio to help with the second week of volunteer training.

On June 21, Mickey, James Chaney, and a new volunteer from New York—Andrew Goodman—drove 40 miles outside of Meridian to speak to leaders from the Mt. Zion Methodist Church. Having agreed to host a Freedom School for the summer, the leaders were severely beaten, and their church had been firebombed.[23]

When the three did not return or call on time, panic began to sweep through the community center. As the clock ticked on, the new volunteers sat nervously in the Freedom Library, with "nothing to do but play ping pong or read and wait for the phone to ring." The missing person protocols that were used when Lester McKinney went missing (see chapter 3) were initiated, although those who really knew what to do were either part of the missing three or still in Ohio.

After speaking with the leaders of the now-destroyed Mt. Zion Church, the three had been driving back to Meridian when they were pulled over by police and arrested. They were then released from police custody at 10:30 p.m., only to be pulled over again minutes later. Accompanied by members of the Ku Klux Klan, the police shot and killed all three.[24]

"These children are Mississippi's best hope," Mickey had written in an earlier report to CORE, stating how the library's story time had attracted a group of toddlers. "They are the ones who, if assisted, can improve most and contribute most."[25]

EATING DIRT

"Patti Miller . . . Community Center . . . Meridian, Mississippi."[26]

Hearing her name called out and matched to that particular town, Patti Miller felt "numb and a bit sick." Miller was at Tougaloo College in Jackson, Mississippi, attending orientation for the second wave of summer project volunteers entering Mississippi. Born and raised in Iowa, she was a music major at Drake University when she saw a leaflet advertising the summer project. Having toured the Deep South the year before, she—like many other workers—"had to come."[27]

She found the community center on 5th Street to be equally as decrepit, filthy, and probably unsafe as the Schwerners had during their first encounter. "As I climbed the stairs and saw the community center for the first time, I was struck with how old and run down the building was," Miller recalled. She also remembers the people inside appeared equally run down, as "no one was particularly friendly as I had expected nor did anyone even seem to notice I was there."[28]

Although she found "everything so new and so strange, and now, so terrifying," she also found the massive library. "Mickey Schwerner and his wife Rita had gone to Meridian several months before," Miller recalled. "Mickey built bookshelves in all of the rooms and then when the books started arriving, they just filled the

Patti Miller and another volunteer from Drake University hold a story time in the Meridian Freedom Library. *Courtesy of Patti Miller.*

shelves with books. So when I worked there, we had lots and lots of books."[29]

Miller jumped right in, conducting story times and teaching arts and crafts. She also took many of the library regulars on trips to local parks and playgrounds. After her first week or two, she noticed that most of the children who attended story time had large bulges of candy in their cheeks. She asked one child about the type of candy he was eating, and he stated it wasn't candy, but dirt. All the children were chewing clumps of dirt. They even showed her the vacant lot where they all got their dirt from.[30]

"The dirt had visible veins of minerals running through it, and the children in their bodies' wisdom, somehow knew that they could get needed minerals from the dirt."[31]

Miller also handed out flyers advertising a memorial march for James Chaney, following the family's private burial of their son. As she joined the hundreds who silently marched through the streets of Meridian, someone began to yell, "White girl," and, "Nigger lover," at her. "Why do you care about a dead black man? You

Daily life inside the Meridian Freedom Library and Community Center. *Courtesy of Patti Miller.*

gonna marry one of them?" That a "white woman in curlers sitting on her porch" could say this within earshot of parents shattered by grief opens another window into what daily life was like for African Americans in Mississippi.[32]

"Damn the movement! I want to go home," Miller wrote mid-August in her personal diary. Not only had the library been receiving more than the usual amount of threatening phone calls, including a bomb threat, but Miller also felt deeply disappointed in seeking help from local churches. Meridian ministers had told her that God "meant for segregation to exist" and that they didn't have time for "inferior Negroes." She did not leave, though, and kept on reading to the young children, teaching arts and crafts, and holding sessions on hygiene for the older ones.[33]

Miller returned to school at the end of August, but not before training another volunteer to carry on her duties.

Books continued to flood into Meridian, even with the end of the summer project. Psychoanalyst Sidney Tarachow donated his own personal library, including numerous titles "by and about Ne-

Volunteer and local students in Meridian. *Courtesy of Patti Miller.*

groes," which were in high demand. A physician from West Chester sent parcels of books for "both adults and children," and *Parent's Magazine* also sent a large package of books.[34]

Talk of changing the name of the Meridian Community Center to the Chaney Goodman Schwerner Memorial Center began as early as July but picked up momentum in the fall of that year. Funds began to be raised by CORE SEDFRE (Scholarship Education Defense Fund for Racial Equality), an architectural firm was contracted, and celebrities such as Jackie Robinson and Steve Allen became closely involved. A large modern center was envisioned, one with a chapel, swimming pool, auditorium, and outdoor terrace.[35]

Rita Schwerner, who must have been sick with grief, wrote to CORE, asking people not to lose sight of the center's civil rights purpose, and to be wary of a "meaningless structure established simply for the vanity of well-meaning but vague and confused outsiders." She also expressed concern for the library she and her husband worked so hard at: "The library should not simply be a room filled with books, but a place where reading is encouraged as both enjoyment and a means of increasing earning potential. . . . Books borrowed must be returned, although I never found fines to be necessary."[36]

"It was hard," wrote a carpenter from California in a letter to the *Nation* dated September 5, 1964. "We suffered from heat, humidity and harassment. One of our cars was firebombed, a dynamite bomb was exploded 30 feet from our building site." The letter was from Abe Osheroff, who—after learning about the summer project—raised $20,000 so he could build a community center for the people of Mileston, Mississippi. With his partner Jim Boebel, the two left their California business behind and spent all summer and most of the fall building the center with the help of local volunteers.[37]

A DIFFERENCE OF AMERICAS

"The building has an assembly hall for 200 people, a library for 10,000 volumes," continued the letter, also mentioning the recently installed kitchen and bathrooms. "The center is now being run by Mr. and Mrs. Lorenzi, a white couple." This was Henry and Sue Lorenzi, who arrived in Mileston at the tail end of the summer project, just as most of the students were returning back to their northern colleges.[38]

The Lorenzis were newlyweds when they arrived, having married each other in June just before Sue's graduation from Stanford.

"Nowhere else on earth is the lunacy of man's abuse of himself so grotesquely underlined by visible evidence of what might otherwise be. And this tragic success is perverting so much that is so lovely and so promising into a sleepless nightmare." The sleepless

Sue Lorenzi walking to the Mileston Freedom House. *Courtesy of Sue Lorenzi Sojourner.*

nightmare was the human rights abuses taking place in Namibia, as reported by Allard K. Lowenstein in the book *The Brutal Mandate*. As one of Stanford's deans, Lowenstein had frequent talks with Sue, who credits his book with "opening her eyes to oppression of blacks." As a recruiter for the summer project, Lowenstein encouraged Sue and her husband to participate. They committed themselves for at least one year.[39]

The two arrived in Mileston in late September, being housed with the Howard family, who owned the soybean field where the community center was being built. They would then move into the loft located in the community center when it was completed. This happened on October 18, when the HCCC (Holmes County Community Center) officially opened.[40]

Four hundred people came to the opening that day, including members of the state police known to harass anyone connected with the Civil Rights Movement. Besides setting up roadblocks and noting the licenses of those who came to the center, they also arrested volunteer John Allen for attempting to take their picture. Stokely Carmichael was also there (of course), and an October WATS report stated that Carmichael "was arrested for interfering with an officer, blocking traffic, and disobeying an officer. He was crossing the street."[41]

"What I hope will be said of this center," carpenter Jim Boebel said to those who came out that day, "is that in the summer of 1964 when white folks in Mississippi were burning down some 30 churches, the Negro folks of Mississippi and their white friends were building community centers." His partner Osheroff hoped the center would be "regarded as an offering from friends in California who as long as Negros are held in bondage in Mississippi, are held in shame and guilt." *The Student Voice* reported on it that day, noting the center had, among other things, a "library containing 7000 volumes donated by friends in the North."[42]

Sue did double duty as both teacher and librarian at the center. She also organized social programs for the community while teaching "a daily kindergarten and once-or-twice-a-week story time in the library." Its impact was immediate, being "a place for people to go and know they would not be turned away because of their skin color."[43]

Butchie Head at the
Mileston Freedom
House. *Courtesy of Sue
Lorenzi Sojourner.*

"The center gives me a good understanding about my life and
I have also learned to read more books," wrote a young resident of
Mileston, Mississippi. "Henry and Sue have tried to train me to
work things out and not look to them for everything." A fellow teen
supported this by writing, "The center is the best thing that the
Negro can have. It gives them a better understanding about life. . . .
It teaches them to read and check out books from the library and
to go get information."[44]

The books, the teaching, and the story times were not the only
things both Lorenzis provided to Holmes County. Having white
skin was also influential. "We weren't used to being around white
people," recalled Sam Epps, whose family frequented the commu-

nity center. "We thought differently but Henry and Sue gave us a whole new demeanor." Famed photojournalist Matt Herron, having arrived for the HCCC grand opening, also noted this interaction, writing, "These kids had never imagined friendship with a white person. It changed their sense of life's possibilities."[45]

Rosie Head, a Mileston resident in her twenties, celebrated her birthday in the center's library. Those in attendance either sat or stood around chatting (or tried to over the loud records being played), played cards, and clanked overflowing glasses to the birthday girl, to freedom, or both. Almost immediately, Sue noticed that "the many books, packed into the totally shelf-lined walls and spilling over into cardboard boxes stacked high along the sides, were being ignored. . . . No one reached up to leaf through any of the books." A difference of Americas was on display. Any party in a library that Sue could recall would have had many attendees "searching and flipping through various books and discussing them with other guests. The shy ones would just read the books outright." In retrospect, Sue thought maybe it wasn't so much that the Mileston

Thelma "Nutchie" Head at the Mileston Freedom House. *Courtesy of Sue Lorenzi Sojourner.*

residents had not grown up with schools and books, but probably "they just knew how to enjoy themselves more."[46]

Referred to as the "dream in a bean field," and "a dream made reality, a reality above price," the HCCC did come with a price. As historian John Dittmer notes, "White residents of Holmes [County] did not take kindly to this invasion by outsiders." The backlash had begun the year before, when Hartman Turnbow, a local farmer, attempted to register to vote. After his registration was denied, the local Klan shot into his home after firebombing it. After he and his family had survived the attempt to kill them (possibly because Turnbow began to return fire), "Turnbow was arrested the following day on charges of arson."[47]

As mentioned above, the community center was the target of bombings while it was being built, and tossed dynamite paired with shootings became more frequent when it was up and running. "Every night," Sue Lorenzi remembers, "armed guards watched the Holmes County Community Center."[48]

It may seem odd to see or hear about guns in a movement based on nonviolence. The ones in Holmes County, as used by Turnbow

Armed guards at the Holmes County Community Center. *Photo by Matt Herron. Courtesy of The Image Works.*

and others, were for self-defense only. Even Dr. King drew a line between "the right to defend one's home" and "nonviolent demonstrations."[49]

Sue's husband Henry was arrested on November 1 and charged with carrying a concealed weapon. Earlier in the day he and two other adults agreed to drive some teenagers from the community center to their homes. The teens had been unable to leave the center without constant police interference. "I was filled with terror for my husband," Sue stated, "and spent a long night alone at the center." Pulled over for a "loud muffler," the police had found a bread knife among the Lorenzis' picnic supplies. Henry was released the following day with all charges dropped, after assuring the judge he had "no longer term plans in the county."[50]

Sue and Henry didn't just stay the full year they had originally committed to—they stayed for five, helping the center evolve into a federally funded Head Start program and renamed the Mileston Head Start Center.[51]

THEY EAT THEIR MISSIONARIES

Ruleville always had it tough.

Located not far from the much-dreaded Parchman Prison Farm, the town was ruled by terror, with a heavy presence of both the Citizens' Council and the Klan. The home and hiding place of Emmett Till's killers, the small town's locals were frequently terrorized at night by Klan members shooting blindly into family homes. African American schools were simply tragic, with "outdated textbooks, nonexistent libraries, and poorly prepared and underpaid teachers." Slavery also still existed, with students going on special field trips to pick cotton. Those not participating were either fined or flunked.[52]

This was reflected in the Ruleville Freedom Library, which was "a tumbledown house at the edge of the black neighborhood . . . two 12-by-12 rooms, a splintering porch, and a crawlspace above." This was the impression Ellen Siegel had, a nineteen-year-old University of New Hampshire student, when she first arrived at what would be Ruleville's Community Center at 820 Quiver Street.[53]

Seven thousand books had arrived in a truck from Chicago, but the police had pulled the truck over as it approached the community center. After confiscating the licenses from the truck's occupants, the police ordered them to open the back trailer for inspection. Project director Charles McLaurin walked over from the center and demanded that the police get a search warrant. This caused some confusion, and after leaving and returning a few times—always without a search warrant—they finally returned the licenses and released the truck. "The police don't know what to do when you insist that they follow legal or constitutional limitations," McLaurin stated while filing a report with the FBI. "They are used to dictatorial methods."[54]

Volunteers and locals both emptied the truck, with Ellen Siegel spending the next week weeding through the donations. While more than half were unsuited for the library, Siegel remembers them having other uses. "Not only did we need to unpack and shelve boxes and boxes of donated books, we also needed to construct the shelves. I remember having planks, but a limited number of shelf supports. Being resourceful and of limited means, we repurposed books we neither approved of or liked (think lots of Reader's Digest), wrapping them in newsprint and stacking them like bricks. In no time at all we had our shelves."[55]

Another volunteer recalls making a table out of an unhinged door, and a blackboard out of a discarded crib headboard. As in other Freedom Libraries, Siegel created a rudimentary Dewey classification, with books arranged by themes such as "Books by and about Negroes," "Literature," "History," "Science," and "Social Sciences." Kirsten Powell, a volunteer from Australia, reported the library "had everything from Nancy Drew to Thomas Mann," although she hoped books by Richard Wright would soon make it to Ruleville. Clipping files were assembled on citizens' rights to use as teaching aids, as a handful of the volunteers were teachers.[56]

Adults arrived for classes early in the morning, turning Siegel and her library into an unofficial day care, with Siegel on diaper duty. The children arrived immediately after school, pouring in and out of the center, and having their first encounter with library books. Siegel held afternoon story times, as well as instructing how

Ellen Siegel reads to youngsters at the Ruleville Freedom Library. *Courtesy of Ellen Siegel.*

to check out books. A *Boston Globe* reporter noted that she "played to her strength as a visual artist. When the children drew only white faces, she encouraged them to imagine African villages, and to express themselves with bold colors and abstract art."[57]

While the Klan would terrorize the center at night, raining down coke bottles and gunshots at the center (with both volunteers and locals waking up to smashed windows and vandalized cars), the Citizens' Council and segregationists operated in the daylight, scoffing and spitting at Siegel as she walked into town to purchase food and supplies. How many African Americans she had been sleeping with appeared to be a favorite question of her tormentors.[58]

Violence also followed Allan Levine, a rabbi who provided counseling to the volunteers at the community center. One of the original Freedom Riders, Levine had already spent time in a Mississippi jail for attempting to integrate a restaurant in Jackson. Since his arrival in Ruleville, the police had twice threatened to kill him at gunpoint, and the Klan had him on an assassination list.[59]

Oddness also visited the Ruleville Center. A lifelong resident of Ruleville named Robert Kent arrived at the center early in July, to make known his views on segregation (he was very much for it). Kent was without violence or animosity, and simply sat chatting with the younger volunteers while exchanging viewpoints. As the evening turned to midnight, the Ruleville police entered the center and arrested Kent under the protest of the SNCC volunteers, who stated their guest "was creating no disturbance, that he was welcome at the center just like any Mississippian." He was charged with being drunk and disorderly and paid a fine of eighteen dollars.[60]

Later in the summer a small group of people calling themselves the Association of Tenth Amendment Conservatives, or ATAC, asked the SNCC to have coffee with them. Since no place would serve African Americans, they instead sat outside the home of Fannie Lou Hamer, and had a tour of the community center. While the group was polite and respectful, the volunteers felt no progress was made in race relations that evening.

Both the Ruleville Public Library and the one in the neighboring community of Indianola not only were segregated but also began to refuse service to Civil Rights Movement volunteers of any color. One volunteer was arrested and held without charges after doing some research at the Ruleville Library, while three volunteers in Indianola were told by the head librarian that "in Africa, they eat their missionaries," before posting a notice stating anyone involved in the movement was banned.[61]

"I don't think she has slept well since she has seen us," joked volunteer David Gerber about the head librarian. Gerber also seemed to think that by restricting the library to tax-paying residents only (as indicated by the posted notice), this would include African Americans. The board, he stated, had felt this was far better than "admitting SNCC workers."[62]

On July 16 all those involved with the community center headed over to a freedom rally in the town of Drew, a mere ten minutes outside of Ruleville. All were arrested and taken to the Drew City Jail. After sending underage minors home to their parents, the police then moved the prisoners to Moorhead County Penal Farm, where the warden there said he would be unable to "insure the safety" of the civil rights workers now in his custody.[63]

Ellen Siegel was one of the arrestees, after the police destroyed the film she had in her camera. After two nights spent "on a grimy mattress," an FBI agent came to interview her, but the agent was more interested in the type of subversive organizations she belonged to back home than her extra-legal arrest. Siegel was released with the others after her parents sent the incredibly high bail money ($4,860), and a higher court would later void the arrests.[64]

Urged to return home, Siegel told her parents she was staying in Ruleville. "I am very happy here."[65]

VICKSBURG: RELATIVELY SAFE

"Well," Shelton Stromquist thought. "That's interesting."[66]

Stromquist had been sitting outside the Freedom Library in Vicksburg, when a car full of working-class teens drove right up to him. "We've been hearing stories in the gas station about people who want to do you folks harm," one of them told Stromquist. "They want to blow this place up." No one knew what quite to make of the messengers, whether they were sincere or just trying to scare people. "I think simplistically they were outcasts in some sense of their own community," Stromquist reported, believing they were acting in good faith.[67]

The Vicksburg Freedom House was located at 1016 Hossley Street, very close to the city's downtown core. "An old kind of rambling structure on a hill on a large lot surrounded by woods," it was truly a multipurpose building, housing "the Vicksburg COFO Project office, Freedom School, living accommodations for six civil rights workers, and the Freedom Library." Bessie Brown—a single mother with seven children—also lived there.[68]

Bryan Dunlap, a volunteer from New York, was to be in charge of the library. After his orientation in Oxford, he arrived to find "the Vicksburg Freedom Library had no books [and] no shelves." By the time the books poured in from the North, well over ten thousand of them, Dunlap had built a "circulation desk and seventy-two feet of shelf space." He didn't realize it at the time, but he had created "one of the best community center libraries in the state." Part of Dunlap's acumen in librarianship undoubtedly came from his father—a professional librarian at New York City College.[69]

A letter to his father reads, "Dad, please send me a copy of the library prospectus" as well as "a book on library cataloging systems and (if possible) a hot pen and white marking tape for putting call numbers on books."[70]

Which also gave him the motivation to visit the Vicksburg Public Library. There he found the history section to "run heavily to books on the War Between the States, and the inevitable stars and bars hangs on a coat hanger frame, beside a small equestrian statue of some Rebel officer, in a corner of the Cataloging desk." "A wretched library" is how he described it in a letter to his grandparents.[71]

Dunlap was a prolific letter writer, and he appeared to write just as many memos and notes mentioning want lists the Vicksburg Freedom Library needed, and especially what they did not need. This last category included "out-of-date books (especially in the sciences), worn-out textbooks in grade school subjects, workbooks, back issues of magazines, outdated reference books; Readers Digest condensed books, [and] any book with badly broken binding, missing pages, etc."[72]

The point about out-of-date books is best illustrated by Fran O'Brien, a volunteer from Oregon's Pacific University. Hoping to teach some of the children history, she grabbed one of the donated textbooks from the library and opened to the sentence "The history of America really begins in England because all Americans come from England."[73]

Of all the towns in Mississippi, Vicksburg was supposed to be different. At his orientation in Oxford, Stromquist recalls that "it was pretty clear that Vicksburg was a different kind of place than a lot of other communities." The expectations were going to be different. The people weren't expecting the same kind of resistance and violence. O'Brien believed this as well. In a letter to her parents, she asked them not to worry about her, for "Vicksburg is a quiet little town." Dunlap also told his own parents that "there have so far been no signs of direct action or reprisals." Those who initially left Oxford were relieved to be sent to "the relatively safe project in Vicksburg."[74]

"There has been no white citizen's council," wrote journalist Drew Pearson, "no Ku Klux Klan." In the same article Pearson mentioned Vicksburg's mayor's statement about how he "went out of his way to protect freedom workers," and how his chief of police would protect all those coming to the city as civil rights workers.[75]

None of this was true, though.

After visiting a couple in their seventies to discuss voter registration, Stromquist learned that after his visit, three truckloads of Klan members "drove up to the house, pulled the older man and woman out on the lawn and beat them and burned a cross in their yard." While waiting for a ride outside the center, Fran O'Brien was kidnapped by four men and severely beaten. All summer saw incidents of violent repercussions from both hooded assailants and unmasked ones, including vehicles chasing and circling people, gas bombs, shootings, stoning of children, and numerous assaults. Economic reprisals, unwarranted arrests, and police brutality also came down on those even indirectly involved with the movement.[76]

But it was the attempted murder of fourteen people that really shattered any notion that Vicksburg was an outlier of safety.

At approximately 2:50 a.m. on Sunday, October 4, a large amount of dynamite was ignited directly below the Freedom House. "A loud prolonged explosion and a flash of light" accompanied the detonation, caving the wooden building in on itself. While the Brown family was asleep, most of the volunteers were awake—either working or just up late talking. Vicksburg was being hammered by heavy winds and intense rain that night, as Hurricane Hilda tracked across the lower part of the state. It would have been next to impossible to hear people crawling under the building (which was on stilts) and placing explosives.[77]

Mrs. Brown and her seven children suffered the worst. An eerie silence loomed after the blast, when the survivors could only hear the rain, and then the crying of the Brown children. Splintered wood and glass had cut Mrs. Brown and one of her daughters in several places. Her two-month-old grandson was bruised from the concussive blast. Her youngest daughter, only two years old, was found buried in the wreckage and had to be dug out. The other children were not physically injured, but "suffered from shock." The remaining six were project staff and local residents, who amazingly survived with little harm.[78]

Later the FBI determined the dynamite had been expertly placed under the building and against the heavy supporting beams, which "should have brought the entire structure down," killing everyone inside.[79]

"But what they didn't know," reported Sheldon Stromquist, who counted himself among the survivors that morning, "what the bombers didn't know is that it [the bomb] was placed directly under freedom school books. The Freedom Library had boxes that were packed floor to ceiling. We think that the reason nobody was killed in that house was because those books absorbed the concussion of the bomb."[80]

All those books, the ones that had poured in from the northern states, "more books than we could possibly use," recalled Stromquist, had "through accidental circumstance prevented a mass killing that October morning. Which is just incredible."[81]

"The pain grows worse with each bombing," wrote Mendy Samstein, a SNCC worker stationed in McComb. "The sound is more anguishing . . . and one's stomach aches with pain and the pain seeps up into the chest and the head and comes out of every pore. . . . The fear and suspense grows—the anguish becomes unbearable." The anguish was little less unbearable in Vicksburg. The books were destroyed, but because of them, no lives were.[82]

As with McComb, the Vicksburg Freedom House wasn't dependent on a building either. Within hours of the blast, the former residents of 1016 Hossley Street carried on pretty much as they always had. Finding the Browns a new place to live was the day's priority, followed by mass meetings in various churches to find a new Freedom House.

Books that weren't destroyed in the blast were ruined by the rain and the careless boots of law enforcement. Dunlap wrote home as usual, outlining his plans and needs to rebuild a new library, and he had an ingenious idea. He proposed a book-for-book swap with supporters in the North. In exchange for a new copy, they would get "a souvenir of the Vicksburg bombing."[83]

A large list of replacement books needed was also included, along with an appeal for Carter Woodson's *Negro Orators and Their Orations,* Robert Kerlin's *Negro Poets and Their Poems,* and Eva Beatrice Dyke's *The Negro in English Romantic Thought.* He also had to break the news that *The Bookman's Guide,* a title his father sent to him via interlibrary loan, was destroyed in the blast.[84]

Disturbed by news of the bombing, the Nassau-Suffolk School Library Association sent a package of new books including titles by Ezra Jack Keats, Louisa Shotwell, Hildegarde Swift, Ann Petry, Jeanette Nolan, and Langston Hughes.[85]

The Vicksburg project was having difficulty finding a new location—no real estate owner was eager to see their property bombed. Any place they did secure they were quickly evicted from before they had a chance to move in. One office was secured, but before anyone could unpack even one crate of books the city's health department evicted them for not having working toilets. A second location had to be vacated as well, after the landlord was threatened with arson.[86]

Anonymous gunshots continued to follow the project, along with increased police harassment, and a new Citizens' Council was being formed. The continued presence of Stromquist, O'Brien, Dunlap, and the others was a constant reminder to Vicksburg officials that their city was not the safe and racially harmonious place they projected it to be. Dunlap reported that the police chief "would like to see us back [home] in Moscow, where we came from."[87]

And then, for a variety of reasons—none of them moral or humane—Vicksburg desegregated its public spaces—including its public library. The Freedom House also converted to a Head Start center (just under three hundred Head Start centers had opened in Mississippi by the summer of 1965, many either working with or replacing the summer project's Freedom Libraries and centers). Right before this shift, Miriam Braverman—a librarian from Brooklyn representing the Friends of the Freedom Libraries—arrived in Mississippi for a type of fact-finding mission and tour. While she found each one "integral to the arsenal of weapons of the nonviolent movement," she was disappointed with her visit to Indianola Freedom Library. It was a burned empty lot, having been bombed earlier that year.[88]

Another shift was happening inside the Civil Rights Movement itself. COFO would dissolve, and the SNCC would experience internal splits. Before this, the movement turned its focus from Mississippi to Alabama, with the dual strategy of bringing literacy and books into a state that "was about to become a raging hell on earth."[89]

Chapter Five

―――――――――――○―――――――――――

Alabama

Books in the Black Belt

SNCC HAD CHOSEN MISSISSIPPI for the summer project for a variety of reasons. Not only did it have the lowest percentage of African Americans registered to vote in the entire country, but also SNCC had been working there since 1961; organizational structure and vital community contacts were already in place. Although the summer of 1964 resulted in thousands of arrests, beatings, and state-sponsored murder, the amount of untold violence visited on the movement volunteers had been expected and prepared for.[1]

Unlike Mississippi, Alabama appeared impenetrable. In direct contrast to its neighboring state, Alabama would only see two Freedom Libraries established. Out of the state's sixty-seven counties, only two would be the focus of SNCC volunteers: Dallas County, which contained the small city of Selma, and Lowndes County, whose county seat was the even smaller city of Hayneville.

It was Jonathan Seigenthaler, Robert Kennedy's assistant and Justice Department representative, who felt Alabama would "become a raging hell on earth" for those in the SNCC about to enter it. "The amount of white anger," Bernard Lafayette Jr.—one of the founding members of the SNCC—noted, "was far above the norm." He had been warned to stay out of Selma altogether, as "the white people were too mean and the black people too scared." The town had routinely been voted down and scratched off lists when brought up as a possible project. Lafayette had ventured into Selma anyway in 1963, where he and his wife were greeted by two Justice Department officials. The Washington men offered both Lafayette and his wife two full scholarships to Columbia University if they would simply leave before getting killed.[2]

Lowndes County was even less welcoming. The history of the county is marked by death and terror for its African American residents. Chronic violence was used "to enforce white supremacy, slavery, peonage, disfranchisement and segregation." Hayneville in particular was "a place where whites could brutalize blacks and their white allies without fear of punishment in the halls of justice." Known better by its familiar moniker "Bloody Lowndes," it was also known as "the Devil's Backyard, "the very heart of darkness," and— echoing Seigenthaler—"worse than hell." Dr. King was warned not to go there, and a seasoned U.S. marshal admitted Lowndes was "no man's land and I am afraid of it."[3]

It is not surprising that the SNCC was extremely worried about sending volunteers, acknowledging that "the decision was Lowndes county was so bad no one would come in there."[4]

ALABAMA LIBRARIES

A bit of history.

The growth of Alabama public libraries mirrored that of Mississippi's. Alabama also had few libraries in the nineteenth century, a fact that did not change during the first part of the twentieth century. In his historical look at Alabama library development, Kenneth R. Johnson found the state to have "many conditions which were not conclusive to a system of good libraries." Even by 1920 "no library was established with tax revenue or by government officials." A survey conducted by the State Department in 1915 concluded "that the majority of Alabamians had no library at all."[5]

Reasons for the state's delayed development in library service are varied, but most point toward the socioeconomic conditions of Alabama's residents. A study by Annabel K. Stephens aptly concluded that "due to conditions of extensive poverty, illiteracy and poor education, and the rural nature of most of its communities, the majority of Alabama libraries were established much later than those in other parts of the country." Johnson's research supports this, finding "extensive poverty led many persons to prefer low taxes rather than libraries." These conditions created a large number of citizens who "possessed little appreciation of the value and pleasure to be derived from reading," creating a "tradition that placed little value on books."[6]

Although Alabama clearly lacked any government-run or tax-funded public libraries, it had a rich history of private citizens, women's clubs, and community organizations that provided public library services. A study of 116 such libraries clearly illustrated just "how highly motivated many of Alabama's citizens were to have a place in their communities where people could come to read, obtain materials for home reading, and meet together to discuss important issues."[7]

All of the historic libraries mentioned above also mirrored Mississippi's unmistakable feature in their services: African Americans were barred from using them. Like other Southern states, Alabama did have its share of segregated libraries, but these also adhered to the "dishonest farce" of separate but equal facilities, providing the typical "scattered, rundown, understaffed and under stocked with books" libraries for African Americans.[8]

Echoing the leadership of the American Library Association, the Alabama Library Association was also not much help. When someone suggested opening up the association to African Americans in 1949, a resounding "no" was voiced. Most were "definitely opposed to the idea," "not ready," and that "the implications were entirely too great." William Stanley Hoole, who sat on the executive council of the association, wanted to know "who is stuffing these Negroes down our throats?" With this overwhelming dissent, the association agreed that "Alabama will do well not to open membership to Negroes."[9]

Getting books into Alabama was going to be just as difficult as it was for Mississippi. The SNCC knew this, and—just like they did in Mississippi—had been working steadfastly behind the scenes since 1963.

Bernard Lafayette Jr. and his wife had turned down the scholarships to Columbia, choosing instead to remain in Selma and try and make some sort of impact. The work ahead of them was as hard and unforgiving as people had said. Lafayette tirelessly canvassed neighborhoods, handed out leaflets, and spoke to any sympathetic person that would listen. He was harassed at every turn, somehow arrested for vagrancy while driving, and his address was published in the local newspaper. His wife, Colia, the only other SNCC member in Selma, attempted to work the phone lines between threatening calls.

The Justice Department had been right. On the night of June 12 Lafayette was to be one of three people killed in a multi-state plot by a faction of the New Orleans Ku Klux Klan. After stopping to help two men with car trouble outside of his Selma residence, Lafayette was badly beaten. He only escaped execution when a neighbor of his ran out with a gun to help. He received eleven stitches and a stay in the hospital.[10]

The violence against Lafayette appeared to only harden those he came to help against him. In other cities and states, churches would at the very least offer limited support or refuge to those struggling for freedom rights, even if some were not that happy about it. The church leaders in Selma were different, politely closing doors on Lafayette when they were not openly hostile to him.

All but one.

St. Elizabeth's Catholic Church, a small structure on the corner of Broad Street and Anderson Avenue, opened its doors to Selma's lone SNCC worker. To be fair, only St. Elizabeth's priest—Father Maurice Ouellet—was willing to help. Most of his parishioners and all of his higher-ups wanted nothing to do with civil rights work, even though Ouellet saw supporting the movement part of his vocation as a priest. Even before Lafayette's arrival, Ouellet was already active in the movement, visiting civil rights workers in jail if they had been arrested or the hospital if they had been beaten. He also took out a full-page newspaper ad stating his full support of the movement, while urging the city to remain peaceful.[11]

His support brought with it unwanted surveillance, threats, phony arrests, and Selma's business leaders asking him to leave their city. The archbishop of his order also ordered him not to participate in any civil rights demonstrations. The stress would find Ouellet hospitalized with bleeding ulcers, but he remained unwavering in his support. After meeting with Lafayette, Ouellet offered the SNCC the use of St. Elizabeth's.[12]

LITERACY IN SELMA

Wishing to offer Ouellet more support, Lafayette traveled to the SNCC office in Atlanta hoping to recruit a summer school teacher named Maria Varela to Selma. Varela was slightly older than most volunteers, having already graduated from college. She also had extensive experience in community organizing, having worked for Chicago's Young Christian Students and New York's Students for a Democratic Society. Although terrified of the South, she joined the SNCC in Atlanta in 1963, teaching at a leadership school for Atlanta's youth who wished to participate or already were participating in the Civil Rights Movement.

Varela was also Catholic, which only increased Lafayette's need for her in Selma. Varela was extremely reluctant to go, knowing of Selma's violent reputation. Lafayette was adamant though, explaining how the Selma movement needed her as much as Father Ouellet did. "None of us are Catholic," he told her. "His bishop is against the Movement, and some in his parish have doubts about his involvement. He needs support from his own."[13]

In a possible move to help her allay her very real fears, Lafayette would send Varela undercover. Although of Latino descent, Varela could be (and often was) mistaken as having white skin, which would make her that much more of a target of hate and violence in Selma. The goal was to have no one know she was connected to civil rights work in any way.

Varela arrived in Selma in October of 1963 and set up in St. Elizabeth's. It was there where she created a weapon to be used against the unforgiving level of white supremacy in Selma: literacy.[14]

What would become known as the Selma Literacy Project was produced by Valera during most of the year at St. Elizabeth's. In the prospectus she created for the project, she clearly states how literacy equals the vote, and how the vote would change everything. This would be one of the most difficult challenges the SNCC would ever encounter.

To administer a literacy test to the very people Alabama had denied education and library services to was the final cruelty in a long line of dehumanizing practices. The long memory of slavery, the Jim Crow laws, and the inherent violence and terrorism that went with it created a generational "fear rooted in feelings of inferiority." Overcoming these psychological barriers only led to real-world ones, including the threat of and actual physical violence (including murder), loss of employment, poisonous snakes dropped on those standing in a voter registration line, arrest for offenses one hadn't committed, and a never-ending list of obstacles "no fiction writer [would] have the temerity to invent."[15]

Even Burke Marshall—the head of the Justice Department's Civil Rights Division—knew that voting for African Americans in Alabama was "more than a legal issue. For it takes courage, patience and massive effort before a significant number of Negro residents are ready to break the pattern of their lives by attempting to register to vote. Promised federal rights again become illusionary."[16]

The Selma Literacy Project was to run concurrent with Mississippi's Freedom Summer. The SNCC was the first to admit that the mere two months was nowhere near long enough for an adult to gain "functional literacy." It was also doubtful that even a committed learner would become proficient enough to pass the voting literacy test, as even post-secondary educated teachers and ministers frequently failed (while uneducated and illiterate whites miraculously always passed).[17]

What the project could do, what it hoped to do, was twofold. The first was to hopefully teach enough reading and writing ability so an adult could at least face the voting registration test. President Johnson had sent federal registrars to Alabama to observe voting practices, and even if one failed (which was practically guaranteed), a count of African American voters was being recorded for future legal action.

The second was to simply bring literacy instruction to those whose own society had prohibited it. This would be a monumental

Selma literacy prospectus by Maria Varela. *Courtesy of Maria Varela.*

task, as "adults who have not learned to read and write as children often believe they are incapable of learning these basic skills." Combine this belief with that emotionally painful stigma of "grown people going back to school," and one can see the difficulty the literacy project would face.[18]

Varela's plan was to use voter registration as a rationale and a way out of this humiliating shame. In her prospectus, she noted, "Voter registration work can legitimate [sic] participation in a literacy program among non-literates and so help to overcome the stigma often attending such programs."[19] Attending voter registration classes could and often did result in many outcomes—the loss of safety, freedom, employment, one's home, and the very real possibility of loss of life—but the loss of dignity was not one of them. If people needed to read and write to get the vote, then they would put up with learning how to.

Regrettably, books and material needed for the literacy project turned out to be wholly unsuitable. Anything available was naturally aimed at children, building on traditional teaching methods that began with basic one-syllable words and then built to a larger vocabulary. This sequential learning method would only frustrate an older adult, who—as the SNCC would later note—"has a varied reading vocabulary with varied reading skills. He may know the word 'addition' but be unable to read the word 'one.' He may be able to half-spell, half-sound out some words but not others." Combine this with the "childish quality" of professionally produced materials, and all the SNCC would be doing was insulting their target group.[20]

Varela and others began to create suitable learning materials—booklets and visual aids—that would build on the level of understanding the adult nonreader may already have, use subject matter that would be more of interest to adults, and most importantly, "assist the adult to learn things about himself and his race that he was never taught." With such a short time the project hoped this type of literacy intervention would spark an interest in lifelong learning, recognizing that regardless of their past or age, they all had "an unlimited ability to change and grow."[21]

By June the Selma Literacy Project was ready. Workshops, training sessions, and fundraising had occupied Varela for most of the spring. Professional educators helped review and outline teaching materials, and the SNCC was able to recruit and prepare four students to conduct the literacy training. "We realized early that a summer was not long enough to deal with all the research problems," the SNCC stated, "but a start had to be made."[22]

The four student teachers arrived in Selma in mid-June, coinciding with the Mississippi summer project, which—in a bit of historical irony—Varela felt was a terrible idea. The logistics of herself and four African American students entering Selma was a monumental undertaking, and she felt it was "madness to think about managing and protecting nearly a thousand white volunteers and the local people who would be endangered by their presence." She wasn't alone in this opinion, feeling that "the summer project seemed like chaos looking for a place to self-destruct."[23]

The summer project in Selma had barely begun when President Johnson signed the historic Civil Rights Bill on July 2 that prohibited "racial discrimination in employment and education and outlawed racial segregation in public places such as schools, buses, parks and swimming pools." In a moment of joyful celebration, Varela's four student-teachers entered the Thirsty Boy Ice Cream Parlour on Broad Street, mistakenly believing federal law would be instantaneously implemented, and that the restaurant would now be desegregated. Instead of ice cream, the local sheriff's cattle prod was slammed against the neck of one of them, and then all four were dragged off to jail.[24]

To bail them out, Varela would have to break her cover. Wearing "the most feminine summer dress" she owned, she went to the jail and tried to arrange their release. Although her Caucasian appearance confused the deputies, the literacy staff would not be released for a few days. But this was the end of the Selma Literacy Project. Not only was Varela a target of hostile law enforcement, but also the literacy staff felt the entire project should take second place to direct action and mass protests. After securing their release, the literacy teachers went home, and Varela relocated to Mississippi.[25]

The aims and goals of the Selma Literacy Project remain one of the most perfect examples of what happens when a population is denied library service. The public library is at its very best serving adult learners—"those who were not privileged to have primary education when they were supposed to." "Library services are of paramount importance to the success of the goals of adult literacy education." Imagine a place where the nonreading adult could find "relevant and useful reading material, organizing them in some order so that the learners can find materials they need without wasting time." The American library has always been "uniquely situated to promote literacy." Without it, African Americans could never hope to "enjoy fair equality of opportunity to participate in the full range of possibilities that America has to offer."[26]

Things began to shift in Selma in early 1965. Dr. Martin Luther King Jr. and the Southern Christian Leadership Conference held a mass meeting there, launching the Selma Voting Rights Campaign. Inspired by King's speech, over one hundred African American schoolteachers marched to the courthouse to protest the literacy test, only to be beaten and dispersed by sheriff deputies. Dr. King himself was later arrested along with 250 others in a later protest outside the courthouse. Five hundred schoolchildren rushed to the courthouse to protest King's arrest, and they, too, were arrested. "This is Selma, Alabama," King wrote in a letter to the *New York*

Times. "There are more Negroes in jail with me than there are on the voting roles." King asked for the nation's support.[27]

More marches, more arrests, beatings, and the murder of twenty-six-year-old Jimmie Lee Jackson by a state trooper resulted in what history would call Bloody Sunday. This was the now-famous march of six hundred people across Selma's Edmund Pettus Bridge, which was met by state and local law enforcement. The violence unleashed on the marchers was as shameful as it was horrific, what reporter David Halberstam would call "America at its ugliest." He would also note "the state of Alabama using its full force to beat and intimidate its poorest citizens, and thereby keep them from being able to participate in the political process."[28]

The press's coverage of the uncontrolled violence combined with Dr. King's requests (he asked the nation to "put on their walking shoes") resulted in hundreds of people from all over the United States arriving in Selma to participate in another march. This second march would bring people who saw the immediate need to support not only the freedom rights of Selma's citizens but also their right to protest peacefully.[29]

ALABAMA'S LARGEST LIBRARY

One of those who came to Selma was Peter Kellman, who would later rent a building, build shelves, and bring an unheard-of twenty thousand books into Selma. The Selma Free Library emerged simultaneously with one in Lowndes County; these would be the only two Freedom Libraries Alabama would see. Neither of them lasted the summer.

Involved with the New England Committee for Non-Violent Action (CNVA), Kellman had been organizing Vietnam War protesters in Washington, DC, when he first heard about Selma's Bloody Sunday. After returning to the CNVA headquarters in Connecticut, the organization sent Kellman to Selma as their representative. As his bus went through New York, the CNVA had arranged for him to stop there and speak with Bayard Rustin—one of Dr. King's closest advisors and one of the movement's greatest behind-the-scenes organizers. Rustin spoke briefly with Kellman, and—fearing for the young New Englander's life—told him not to go.[30]

Kellman went anyway.

His first assignment was putting up and taking down the tents for those participating in the four-day and fifty-mile march from Selma to Montgomery. Besides working in chronic rain and mud, Kellman and others would "line up shoulder to shoulder and look for bombs." Only after they did this would the National Guard go over the ground with bomb detectors. As the marchers arrived in Montgomery, Kellman's job was to remind the more overexcited ones not to return fire (verbally) to the counter-protesters screaming racial epithets.[31]

While no violence occurred, and President Johnson responded by signing the Voting Rights Act, Alabama was still reluctant to accept change. Kellman accompanied Selma residents lining up at the courthouse to attempt to register, only to have a policeman attack him with a cattle prod.[32]

It was called the Selma Free Library.

It was created in the summer of 1965 by a handful of civil rights movement workers, who—exactly like other libraries in Alabama's history—were responding to a community need. The Selma Free Library came into existence through the efforts of Kellman, Charles Fager, Doris Smith, and Dennis Coleman. The library itself was located in a storefront at 801 First Avenue, rented to them by a local mailman who lived next door with his family. It was just down the street from Selma University.

Its sources of funding were as disparate as the people who ran it. Fager recalls "a local black men's fraternity or lodge agreed to pay the rent." Other sources of finances possibly came in from the SNCC and SCOPE (Summer Community Organization and Political Education). Kellman had hoped to get some of the money earmarked by President Johnson for the war on poverty. He remembers: "I did try to make a trip to Washington, to get some poverty money from Lyndon Johnson's poverty program. One of the reasons that it existed was because of the Civil Rights Movement . . . and there was money for things like libraries [and] bookmobiles. I visited a number of bureaucrats in Washington but I wasn't able to get us any funding."[33]

A slightly older Peter Kellman stands in front of what was once the Selma Free Library. *Courtesy of Peter Kellman.*

Kellman was the one who actually designed and built all the shelves for the library. He recalls: "My thing was I was into building things, and I pretty much figured out, you know the design and did a lot of the work and built all the bookcases, and the bookcases were made of like 2×12s; we had a lot."[34]

As well as the finances, the donation of books and materials came from varied sources. After the nation witnessed or read about the events of Bloody Sunday, concerned Americans began to send care packages to Alabama. SCLC (Southern Christian Leadership Conference) field staff member Bruce Hartford recalls that "people in the north sent a massive amount of food, clothing, and books to Selma. We ended up with thousands of books that we had no idea what to do with because all our energies were focused on voter registration rather than freedom schools and libraries."[35]

These donations were by no means the only ones to fill the Selma Free Library. Charles Fager was instrumental in a successful book drive for the library. He recalls that "many thousands of books were collected and shipped to Selma by supporters mainly around San Francisco (I had met some of them and encouraged this idea)."[36]

Northern colleges also sent book donations, including Antioch College in Ohio and San Francisco State College. Dennis Coleman has stated that "book donations came from a wide variety of sources which were heavy on the academic side." During the previous year in Selma, the SNCC had organized a literacy project. It is possible that any books used then may have also been donated for the library to use.

This small group of volunteers unintentionally created one of the largest public libraries in all of Alabama. In a letter sent on August 12, 1965, to San Francisco State College, Charles Fager reported that the library "presently numbers 18,000 volumes, rivaling in the size any in western Alabama and easily bettering them in quality." Peter Kellman confirms this number: "It was huge! I am trying to remember. . . . The number 20,000 sticks in my mind. I remember that one time we checked out the different libraries in southwestern Alabama and it was the largest in terms of books; no one had any more books than the Selma library did."[37]

While the sheer number of books reported here may seem fanciful, these numbers reflect what the Freedom Libraries in Mississippi had in 1964. Cook found their collections "ranged from a few hundred volumes to more than 20,000." Also, by the summer of 1965, the SNCC's Atlanta office had been swamped with donations numbering "between 100,000 and a quarter of a million books."[38]

After fifty years, what exactly those shelves contained remains unknown; no document has surfaced that lists the exact items found in the Selma Free Library. Fortunately, memories of those who set up and worked at the library are still accessible. In keeping with the Civil Rights Movement, "the collection was strong on Negro authors," and "heavy on the academic side." Peter Kellman believes there "were a fair amount of academic books and a large section on Black History and Black Writers."[39]

"The ones that were the most popular were James Baldwin's *The Fire Next Time* and a few of his other books . . . and one of the most popular books was Fanon's *The Wretched of the Earth*. We got a lot of books from the universities, and they were philosophy and those kinds of books, for courses, but there were also a lot of the books from the English department, so it wasn't just academic textbooks. There were a lot of novels, autobiographies and things that people would probably read while in college."[40]

No library can function if its collection is not organized in a systematic way, and the Selma Free Library was no exception. Dennis Coleman recalls all the books as having been "cataloged and shelved." In his letter to San Francisco State College, Charles Fager informed them that "the collection covers every category in the Dewey Decimal System and is being organized along professional library lines." Although the Dewey Decimal Classification may have been covered, it was not employed in its typical fashion. "We didn't do the Dewey Decimal System," recalled Peter Kellman. "We did it by topic: philosophy was 'WHY' because that is what philosophy is about, the question why." He also stated that biography would be labeled "WHO," geography "WHERE," and history "WHEN."[41]

One of the most fascinating yet telling aspects of the library was the community it served. Located on the same street as Selma University, a surprising number of students favored the Selma Free Library over their own institution's library. Bruce Hartford stated that "SU had recently built a new library building with shelf space for (I think) around 50,000 books . . . but most of the shelves were empty." Peter Kellman confirms this, writing the university "was right down the street from us. They had a new library building but very few books and many of their students used our library."[42]

While the library's overriding raison d'être was to provide Selma's African American community with "the first meaningful contact with books and libraries," the city of Selma already had a public library, one that had desegregated two years earlier.

SELMA CARNEGIE LIBRARY

Research by Toby Patterson Graham clearly illustrates the heroic efforts of Patricia Blalock, who was appointed director of the Selma Carnegie Library in 1963. At great risk to her career and livelihood, Blalock made desegregating the library her first priority. She was successful, and on May 20, 1963, the Selma Carnegie Library opened its doors to all races.[43]

A full two years later, volunteers at the Selma Free Library recall the African American residents of Selma still referred to it as "the white library." Dennis Coleman clearly recalls that "Selma had a library but children in the Negro schools felt a little intimidated using it." As part of her desegregation stance, Blalock was forced to accept the Selma board's insistence on "vertical integration"—the inane practice of removing a library's furniture, to "prevent white and black patrons from sitting together." It appears this practice was still in effect in 1965.[44]

Whatever constraints Blalock was forced to put up with, it appears she felt no ill will or competition from the Selma Free Library. Peter Kellman remembers Blalock referring people to the Freedom Library: "I remember one time some white kids came, young people, because librarians there didn't have a book and they thought we might have it. So they came, and that was the only time I ever remember anyone white from Selma coming."[45]

The constant chaos that often characterized the Mississippi Freedom Libraries was seen in Alabama as well. Kellman remembers that "there were a lot of kids from the neighborhood who would hang out there. They would always be stopping by, and because the movement was still in progress, there was a lot of talk. It wasn't comparable to the library where I lived or had lived. . . . It was a center of discussion; all kinds of things were talked about."[46]

Similar to other civil rights initiatives in Alabama, the goal of the volunteers was to have the library turned over to the residents of Selma. In another letter to San Francisco State College, Patricia Fager wrote, "We want the library to be turned over to the local people as soon as possible. . . . We are training several girls to catalog and take care of the library in general." A separate report confirms this, stating, "Local girls are being trained to catalogue and operate the Library, also they can take it over when it is finally located in a permanent home."[47]

It remains unclear to what exact date the Selma Free Library continued in operation. Civil rights projects usually lasted until summer's end, as most volunteers needed to return to college and university.

When the library dissolved, what happened to its collection? Initially the collection was turned over to the library's neighbor, Selma University. This seemed only natural, as the library workers clearly remember the students from there using the Freedom Library. However, the administration of the university didn't want any items from the Freedom Library. Bruce Hartford stated, "The college trustees were afraid to have anything to do with the Freedom Movement and were deeply suspicious of the radical ideas that might be contained in books from the North, so they rejected the offer."[48]

"In the end," Kellman stated, "the library was turned over to a group of Black Librarians in Dallas County, and I think they divided up the books among their libraries." He also profoundly stated that "part of the [civil rights] struggle was to get control of your past away from those who would define you; those who put you in a subservient position to begin with. I think that is one reason why the libraries were so important."[49]

Also mirroring Mississippi, fear hung over everything. "The fear never left you," Kellman stated. "We didn't have cars or anything like that. We didn't have money. We had to figure out a way to go where you were exposed the least to traffic. One thing we did a lot was get to the railroad tracks and walk down them, or try to figure out just how to stay in black neighborhoods. Never walk on highway 80—that was a constant because our friends were killed. So the fear is always there. It never left. It was one of the toughest things to deal with." Even on his bus trips to Washington, DC, to try and get funding for the library, Kellman was followed and harassed the entire way.[50]

GUNNED DOWN IN HAYNEVILLE

That he had come to Alabama on vacation, and not as a civil rights worker, may have been little comfort to Richard Morrisroe as he sat sweltering in the Hayneville City Jail. Having been arrested with teenage protesters in neighboring Fort Deposit, Morrisroe had been transferred to Hayneville with nineteen others. Although the jail was overcrowded with overflowing toilets and lice-infested mattresses, Morrisroe was in remarkably high spirits. "This is like a retreat," he told a visitor. "Lots of time to read." His cheerful attitude was no doubt part of his character, but also may have been because he had been to Alabama, and jail, before.[51]

Hailing from Chicago, Father Richard F. Morrisroe was the parish priest at Saint Columbus, a large Catholic church located in the city's Park Manor area. His congregation was entirely African American. As a seminary student, Morrisroe had been deeply moved by "activist priests" who spoke out and protested against racial segregation. Now he had become one himself. Not only had he requested to serve at Saint Columbus, but he also joined the Chicago Area Friends of the SNCC, and organized protests against Chicago's segregated school system.[52]

He was also part of the Chicago Catholic Interracial Council, who sent thirty-four members to Selma when Dr. King requested

Richard Morrisroe in 2015. *Photo by Natalie Ammons.*

help after Bloody Sunday. Morrisroe stayed in Selma for more than a week, helping out the local marchers and those trying to register at Selma's courthouse.[53]

Upon returning to Saint Columbus, Morrisroe was "more deeply committed to the cause of racial justice" than before. It was not long after his return that he was arrested for demonstrating against Chicago's city-wide school segregation. The Church was not amused by his arrest. Morrisroe was charged with "neglecting his duties" and was fined a month's pay.[54]

While his superiors were upset with him, his congregation was not. Viewing him as "one of their own," Morrisroe stated, "They inspired me to want to know more about their history and their community, their points of origin." When his vacation days began in August, Morrisroe departed once again from Chicago to Selma. He would arrive not as a civil rights protester, but as a tourist, one hoping to visit and make connections with the friends and family of his Saint Columbus parishioners.[55]

He stopped in Birmingham to pay his respects at the 16th Ave. Baptist Church, the site where the four young girls had been murdered by the Klan. While there he met—you guessed it—Stokely Carmichael. With Carmichael was Jonathan Daniels—an Episcopal seminary student from New Hampshire. Daniels agreed to give Morrisroe a guided tour of the dreaded Lowndes County. Hearing that Carmichael was visiting a Freedom Library in Hayneville, Morrisroe gave him his personal Bible to donate to the library. The three of them then drove on to Selma together, and then departed for Lowndes the following day.[56]

"This Saturday. Aug. 14th at 9 a.m. there will be a demonstration in Ft. Deposit, Lowndes Co. Ala," Stanley Levinson wrote to federal authorities in Washington, DC, hoping they would send either the FBI or National Guard to safeguard the demonstrators. "Klan is very active in area." While the planned demonstration was originally to be about voting rights, a large number of teenagers had shown up, ready to picket local businesses. The SNCC did not want the young people to protest, fearing an "open graveyard" as counter-protesters lined the streets with chains, bats, and guns.[57]

Carmichael and Daniels worked long and hard to get a commitment of nonviolence from the teenagers, no matter what happened to them during the demonstration. This was no easy thing, as these young people had grown up watching Jim Crow abuses rain down on their parents and grandparents, and returning violence appeared to be the appropriate response. The teens who relented would be allowed to march, only after surrendering pens and pencils, long nail files, and the odd pocket knife.[58]

While it remains unknown if they were responding to Levinson's warning or not, federal agents did arrive at Fort Deposit. They weren't there to protect the marchers, though, just to warn them of the danger and ask them to call it off. The teenagers ignored the warnings, feeling it was just another form of racial intimidation. They would march anyway.

Although he had not come to Alabama to demonstrate, there was no way Morrisroe was going to let the young people march alone. He and Daniels joined the teens, noticeably sticking out with their white skin and clerical collars. Daniels's good nature and humor combined with Morrisroe's calm demeanor gave the young people of Fort Deposit the reassurance that they were doing the right thing.[59]

This protest against the local Jim Crow business practices lasted all of sixty seconds. Scores of law enforcement surrounded the marchers and arrested everyone on sight. The demonstrators were taken to the Fort Deposit jail and, after processing, were transferred to the larger Hayneville on the back of a garbage truck.

Morrisroe, Daniels, and the other arrestees were greeted in Hayneville by Stokely Carmichael. Although he had not demonstrated, he had been arrested anyway on a bogus traffic charge. Carmichael would make bail, but the rest stayed locked up for six days with no fans, working toilets, showers, or changes of clothes. Despite the infested mattresses and the inedible bug-laden food, visitors reported that "morale was high" among the prisoners. Daniels was cheery as always, and Morrisroe—as mentioned above—was happy to be reading, working his way through Meyer Levin's *The Fanatic*, John J. Considine's *The Church in the New Latin America*, and Richard Wright's *Native Son*.[60]

Then, as quickly as they were arrested, they were all released. Numerous people and organizations had been working on securing their release, but it came down to the mayor of Fort Deposit, who—after learning that his city might face federal charges of violating the prisoners' civil rights—told the authorities in Hayneville to simply release everyone. It turned out not to be simple, as the prisoners did not want to leave.[61]

No one had paid their bail, no lawyer was on hand to secure their release, and nobody from the SNCC was there to greet them. The SNCC Security Handbook was clear about leaving jail, and foremost on everyone's mind was what happened to Schwerner, Goodman, and Chaney when they were suddenly released from jail (see chapter 4). Refusing to leave, they were eventually marched outside at gunpoint.[62]

Filthy, malnourished, and dehydrated, the group of twenty huddled under some tree shade trying to figure out where the closest phone was. Daniels spotted Varner's Cash Store across the street from them, and suggested soda and ice cream were in order. He and Morrisroe accompanied two teen girls to the store—seventeen-year-old Ruby Sales and nineteen-year-old Joyce Bailey. The four made it as far as the store's front steps.

The first shotgun blast was aimed at Ruby Sales, but Daniels shoved her out of the way and absorbed the blast at point blank range in the chest. He was dead before he hit the ground. Morrisroe had a death grip around Joyce Bailey's hand, dragging her to safety as he ran back to the courthouse. The second shotgun blast tore into Morrisroe's lower back, knocking his body forward onto the hard pavement.[63]

The shooter came out of the Cash Store and stood over both bodies, waving his shotgun at the now scattered and cowering teenagers. He then got in his car and drove away. The stillness of the moment was quickly broken with the sound of horrific moaning. Morrisroe was still alive. The teens moved him out of the street into the shade behind a building and waited with him until help arrived. While he would undergo numerous surgeries and eventually recover, Morrisroe would never have the same mobility again, and "golf, basketball, roller-skating with young and old in the parish gymnasium, even walking" had become "difficult or impossible."[64]

The shooter went through a show trial weeks later, only to be acquitted on all charges. Bogus evidence of Daniels being sexually involved with Ruby Sales, and that he had brandished a knife while Morrisroe held a gun at the Cash Store was presented by various witnesses, and apparently accepted as fact by the jury. Where they would have got the weapons having been just released from jail or the improbability of the two ever carrying weapons were questions left unanswered at the trial. The only thing law enforcement found at the scene were the books Morrisroe had been reading. His personal Bible he had donated to the Hayneville Freedom Library.[65]

It is there to this day.

One overriding characteristic of the Hayneville Freedom Library is the simple fact that it existed at all. This small Alabama town is the county seat of Lowndes County, which also encompasses the surrounding towns of White Hall and Fort Deposit.

Baby Narrowly Escapes Ala. Nightriders Shots
Nightriders in racially tense Hayneville, Ala., shot through the home of a family of twelve and the house next door. Bullets ripped through a window and the crib where Mrs. Pattie Mae McDonald's year-and-half-old son, Walter, had been sleeping only minutes before. A few minutes prior to the shooting, one of the other McDonald children had changed Walter's diaper and kept the baby in bed with her in another room. The blasts tore through the living room wall and ledge. More blasts from a shotgun ripped through the bedroom where Mrs. McDonald slept with her husband, Leon, whose job of erecting telegraph poles often keeps him away from home. The shooting might have occurred, Mrs. McDonald told JET, because she had rented a two-room house to the Student Nonviolent Coordinating Committee (SNCC) for a library and "they (white folks) must have thought I was boarding civil rights workers." The house next door that was also shot into is the residence of her father, Sam Ansley.

Jet Magazine September 23, 1965, issue.

Mrs. McDonald watches as daughter Shirley Ann points to holes in living room wall where bullets went through house.

As mentioned above, the SNCC worried about sending volunteers, acknowledging "the decision was Lowndes County was so bad no one would come in there." Conversely, Stokely Carmichael wanted to go there because of its violent and sinister history. "If they [SNCC volunteers] could help crack Lowndes," he said, "other areas would be much easier." The Hayneville Freedom Library was created for this very purpose.[66]

Jeffries notes that SNCC activists held discussions on African American history "at the freedom library they established in Hayneville during the summer." The library was located at 123 Cemetery Road, an unpaved dead end just north of Hayneville's downtown core.[67]

The Hayneville Freedom Library operated in the home of Pattie Mae and Leon McDonald. This put them in severe physical danger. In his ten-year research project on the county, Jeffries noted: "Pattie McDonald, a forty-four-year-old homemaker and the mother of several young children, recognized early on the value of parallel institutions, including the need for freedom library. This prompted her to let SNCC use the small two-room house that sat unoccupied just behind her modest Hayneville home."[68]

Almost immediately, harassing phone calls, stalking, and death threats soon plagued the McDonald family. And then there was the September 1 incident (described in the introduction), in which the Klan riddled the McDonald home with bullets. This attempted murder of a family of twelve went unreported in the news, and uninvestigated by law enforcement. Only *Jet Magazine* in Chicago found the story worth publishing.

The McDonalds' son, Willie James McDonald, was instrumental in the library's beginnings:

> I was the one that started it at the time. I found a board, probably 1×6 maybe 5 feet long, and I had some paint, and I painted Freedom Library on it, and I put it over the door, and we put the books inside. It [the library itself] was made from used lumber. When they first started building the interstate system, my dad would get off work and we would get used lumber. He would haul it home on the back of his boss truck, and in the evenings and on the weekend we constructed the building.[69]

As with all Freedom Libraries, the collection was donated. Willie McDonald recalls, "All the books were donated from Tuskegee University, which was called Tuskegee Institute at the time." Unfortunately, no titles are remembered, no list exists, and the number of items the library possessed is also unknown. Not only had the students from Tuskegee donated the books, but they also volunteered daily at the library. Willie McDonald remembers: "At that time we had students come down from the Tuskegee Institute, which was in Macon County, they would come down to Lowndes County after school, and they would tutor the students in Lowndes County."[70]

McDonald also recalls Stokely Carmichael using the library, as "his name went down in the history books." Carmichael had great affection for the residents of Hayneville, and he was dedicated to making "it a fit place for human beings."[71]

Pattie Mae McDonald and author in 2013. She and her son Walter still live at the home, which housed the Freedom Library. *Author's photo.*

"My mother does have one book that was left. It was a Catholic Bible, and we are not Catholic, but they had two Catholic priests that were gunned down in Hayneville, and they had given my mother a book and it has a SNCC stamp inside it."[72]

After the September 1 shooting of their home, the McDonalds dissolved the Hayneville Freedom Library. Pattie Mae McDonald burned the library collection, in an attempt to save the lives of her children. According to Willie McDonald, "And all the books, after it was all said and done, my mother burned the books, and the only reason she didn't burn this particular book was because it was a Bible. Now mother isn't Catholic, but that is the word of God and that is the only book left from the library."[73]

The Hayneville Freedom Library and the Selma Free Library both operated in an atmosphere of terror. In Hayneville, the Mc-Donalds knew this fear all too well. Before the shooting in September, they were under constant threat: "Word reached them . . . that Leon McDonald, Pattie's husband, was the focus of an assassination plot. The two white men who stalked him every morning as he walked to catch his ride to work and every evening as he returned home lent credence to the rumors. In addition, during the middle of August, the McDonalds repeatedly spotted a pair of white men—perhaps the same duo that had been shadowing Leon—stalking out the freedom library, and friends informed them that whites were planning to bomb their home."[74]

The failed Selma Literacy Project and the two Freedom Libraries clearly illustrated the amount of racial horror faced by the SNCC and the people they were there to help. "Alabama was extremely dangerous," a movement worker reported prior to the events of 1965. "Selma was just brutal." And as discussed above, Hayneville was characterized as a "terrorist stronghold" long before the shootings of Daniels and Morrisroe. Running a library is an arduous task under ideal conditions: the courage to run one under these conditions remains one of the great untold stories of the Civil Rights Movement.[75]

Although President Johnson signed the Voting Rights Act on August 5 of that year, it would not be the conclusion to the movement he and many, many others had hoped for. The marches, boycotts, and demonstrations did not go away, and Dr. King did not "go home" as the President asked (told) him to. The SNCC was also experiencing a tremendous internal shift, one that favored African American participation only. "Black Power" was a new phrase—taken from Stokely Carmichael's work in Lowndes County—and would begin to be adopted by a more militant and assertive SNCC.[76]

The next Freedom Library to appear would be up north, in Philadelphia. As Morrisroe's protest work in Chicago illustrates, the denial of freedom rights was in no way limited to the Deep South. Libraries were no exception, and a former SNCC worker would open up a Freedom Library unlike any other.

Chapter Six

———————○———————

Philadelphia
Books by and for Black People

IT SHOULD HAVE BEEN a routine call.

It was almost 9:30 on the night of August 28, 1964, when two Philadelphia policemen were dispatched to where Columbia Avenue crossed 22nd Street. A Buick had stalled in the middle of the intersection, backing up traffic on both streets. Upon arriving, the police found the vehicle was in perfect working condition, but—in the middle of a heated argument with her husband—the driver refused to move it. After refusing to either move the car out of the street herself, or let her husband do it, the woman was ordered out of the car. This too she refused, so one of the policemen grabbed her arms and pulled her out of the car, placing her under arrest. She punched, kicked, and bit the officer as he struggled to get handcuffs on her.[1]

As he placed her into the back of his partner's patrol car, a bystander yelled, "You wouldn't manhandle a white woman like you did this lady," before punching the arresting officer in the back of the head. That was all it took. The two policemen called for backup as the growing crowd shouted at them, beating their car with bottles and bricks. Other officers soon arrived in numbers large enough to disperse the hostile crowd, and a horrible rumor spread throughout the city that the police had beaten a pregnant woman to death. Or to be more precise, "a black pregnant woman had been beaten to death by a white policeman." This rumor caused the city to erupt, and rioters burned cars, smashed windows, and looted and destroyed businesses along Columbia Avenue and the surrounding area for the next three days. It would result in thousands of arrests, two deaths, hundreds wounded, and property damage well into the millions. As the *Washington Times* would later report, "When the chaos ended, three days later, hardly a store in the business district had its windows intact."[2]

Incredibly, one storefront was not touched—a small storefront calling itself the Philadelphia Freedom Library. Located at 2064 Ridge Avenue, it was only one street over from where the riot started. Out of all the buildings, it had somehow escaped the city's rage that weekend. Much of the reason it had been spared had to do with the person running it: John Elliot Churchville.

Looted stores after the Columbia Avenue Riot. Only the Freedom Library was spared. *Courtesy of Temple University Libraries, Special Collections Research Center.*

Born and raised in Philadelphia, Churchville was an accomplished jazz musician until one night in 1962 when he met Malcolm X in Harlem. Stirred by Malcolm's commitment to African American rights, he joined the SNCC and soon found himself working in Georgia and Mississippi. Working in voter registration, Churchville was different than most of the SNCC volunteers, as he was a Black Nationalist. He did not believe in the Civil Rights Movement's goal of creating an integrated society. He did not believe in nonviolence. Yet he also didn't believe in using his "ideology as an excuse not to go to work."[3]

He engaged in voter registration drives in southwest Georgia, finding himself harassed by police and arrested for vagrancy. He also clashed with the SNCC's leadership regarding interracial work groups. Churchville felt the African Americans they contacted would typically defer to the white volunteer, undermining the entire purpose of the movement. The SNCC in no way agreed with him, but they did allow Churchville to canvass neighborhoods with African American volunteers only.

For the SNCC workers, southwest Georgia has been characterized as "mean and nasty and hard," with "terrible violence." Churchville recalls that he "had never been so scared." As bad as it was, the SNCC sent a lot of their staff and volunteers to Mississippi due to the brutal violence occurring there leading up to Freedom Summer. Churchville was among the staff transferred.

Assigned to the town of Greenwood (see chapter 4), Churchville took on a different aspect of voter registration. Instead of canvassing, he began to teach literacy to the would-be voters. Similar to Alabama, Mississippi was using a literacy exam to exclude African Americans from voting. This exam required voter registration applicants to "to transcribe and interpret a section of the state constitution and write an essay on the responsibilities of citizenship." This work had a marked effect on him, sparking what would become a lifelong passion for teaching.[4]

"It was an impossible situation," Churchville recalls, noting the difficulty lawyers and legal scholars have understanding the Constitution. Much like his Black Nationalism beliefs, he felt impossible situations were not an excuse to give up. He recalled thinking,

"I'm here right now. These folks are here right now. I'm going to give them the best I got. I'm going to encourage them. I'm going to help them." Knowing few, if any, would pass, he told his students to "walk, put one foot in front of the other. Don't think about the outcome. Don't worry about the end of the road. Just take steps."[5]

As much as he was committed to civil rights work, the SNCC just wasn't a good fit for Churchville. He formally quit and left Mississippi for Atlanta. Here he officially joined the Nation of Islam, and befriended Jeremiah Shabazz—Malcolm X's brother-in-law. Much like the SNCC, Churchville bristled under the Nation of Islam as well, wondering why he couldn't focus on helping the poorest people in Atlanta instead of selling the Nation's *Muhamad Speaks* newspaper.

Shabazz was soon transferred to Philadelphia, and he offered Churchville the job of being his personal secretary at the growing Philadelphia mosque. Happy to be returning to his hometown, Churchville arrived only to be told there was no job for him after all. Since not much appeared to deter him, Churchville wondered what he could do that would combine his love of teaching and civil rights work to help instill racial pride in his hometown. He came up with what he felt was the perfect solution: a Freedom Library.[6]

PHILADELPHIA FREEDOM LIBRARY

"The idea of establishing a Freedom Library," Churchville wrote, "was conceived out of the expressed need of the Negro community in North Philadelphia to find a rich and meaningful identity." Typing out a document he called "General Statement," Churchville identified what he felt was the most pressing problem facing African Americans—their feelings of "worthlessness," "self-hatred," and "the damaging psychological effect on people who had nothing good to believe about themselves except they helped to build America as slaves."[7]

Improving people's views of their own history while involving them in the community became the driving force behind the library. In a type of mission statement, Churchville noted the library's "use by the community would instill racial pride." He also stated that "its base is broad enough to attract and involve Negroes from every social stratum in a positive and active way," and that "it would become a logical extension into the community via young people." Having a real and physical building that the community could call its own would help "tackle the self-hate and identity ambivalence" that appeared to most northern Philadelphians as unescapable.[8]

The General Statement was enough to convince the Dolfinger-McMahon Foundation to give Churchville a grant for $1,200, which he used to secure a storefront he located on Ridge Avenue, tucked between a barber shop on one side and a bar on the other. Jeremiah Shabazz—now going by Jeremiah X—was also enthusiastic about the library. He was able to donate tables and chairs from the Philadelphia mosque, and help Churchville solicit book donations.[9]

While appreciative of all the help Jeremiah X and the Nation of Islam were providing, Churchville himself was no longer a member. Malcolm X had left the Nation earlier that spring, forming the Organization of African American Unity. Finding this new group much more in line with his worldview, Churchville left the Nation and joined the OAAU. In continued support of Malcolm X, he hung a photo of him in the library's front window.

Having survived the riot earlier that year, the library and Churchville himself almost did not survive this. "If you got out of the Nation of Islam and followed Malcolm," Churchville recalled, "you were writing a death sentence for yourself. You were going to get yourself hurt." Fortunately, his friendship with Jeremiah X spared not only his life but also the library as well. The worst that happened was a Nation of Islam cadre came to the library and took back all the tables and chairs they had donated. Jeremiah X remained worried, though, and even appealed to Churchville's mother to have her son "not continue with this stuff."[10]

Unfazed by the removal of furniture, Churchville joined forces with the Northern Student Movement (NSM). Originally created to financially support the SNCC, the NSM had recently turned its concern to its own northern communities. The director of the NSM was William Strickland—an ex-marine who was eager to work with

Churchville. Noticing a small crowd of teens always peering in the windows out of curiosity, Strickland recruited them to help clean up inside and repair broken chairs someone had located. "There was great excitement at the prospect of building a place of our own."[11]

Strickland was instrumental in acquiring books for the library, bypassing publishers and booksellers by writing directly to the authors themselves. A letter to James Baldwin dated August 12, 1964, reads: "We are launching a new project in Philadelphia called the NSM Freedom Library. The Freedom Library will be composed of books by and about Negroes. . . . We cannot afford to buy the books to stock the library and I am wondering if you could suggest persons or organizations to whom we might appeal for books." Strickland signed off by expressing his gratitude, and how he had been unable to see *Blues for Mr. Charlie* (a play of Baldwin's) as tickets had been sold out. Similar letters went out to Maxine Greene, Sylvester Leaks, Andrew Norman, and John Oliver Killens.[12]

As with other Freedom Libraries, no book lists have survived. A list of recommended titles dated October 7, 1964, is still existing though and lists the following titles: *They Showed the Way: Forty American Negro Leaders* by Charlemae Hill Rollins; *My Dog Is Lost* by Ezra Keats and Pat Cherr; *My Mother Is the Most Beautiful Woman in the World* by Becky Reyner; *Prudence Crandall: Woman of Courage* by Elizabeth Yates; and *Frederick Douglass: Slave-Fighter-Freeman* by Arna Bontemps. Two book lists from the New York Public Library were also recommended: "Books about Negro Life for Children" by Augusta Baker, and "The Negro: A List of Significant Books" by Dorothy Homer. Though it is unknown what exact books made up the library's collection, it was reported to have "2000 books by Negroes and/or about Negroes."[13]

"The more I investigate books for the 'freedom library,'" opens an undated and unsigned letter to Churchville, "the more impressed I have become with the difficulty of obtaining some." The anonymous author suggests approaching libraries, college professors, and ministers who are often given free books and may be willing to pass these on. Any books worthy of note, though, are going to have to be bought. "I have been trying to get Wright's *Twelve Million Black Voices* for the last couple of years without success."[14]

By the fall of 1964, the library was featured in the September 6 edition of Philadelphia's *Sunday Bulletin*. Reporter James Smart was curious about why the building was still intact "in the midst of the area bashed by the rioters in North Philadelphia." Smart reports, "Broken stores near it are covered with plywood now, and policemen lounge in small groups down the block. On the window of the empty store are neat gold decal letters which says, 'NSM Freedom Library.'"[15]

Finding Churchville inside, Smart asked him about the library's purpose. "When people don't have any sense of themselves, any positive identity, we feel this is the cause of antisocial behavior. If we can create in the Negro community a feeling of identity, based on knowledge of history and on self-improvement, it will help end antisocial behavior." "Whatever I do is helping myself," Churchville told Smart, "because I still live in this community."[16]

Possibly because of Smart's article, another group came to interview Churchville: the FBI. Arriving early enough one morning to find him alone, the agents wanted him to give them any information he had on James Forman. Churchville became angry. He felt the agents could clearly see what he was trying to accomplish with the library. What incensed him the most was the FBI's hands-off approach when he had been working in the Deep South. "When we called you when people were being lynched, and you said you couldn't do anything, but you have time now to try to pin something on a guy who hasn't broken any laws yet?" Clearly at an impasse, the agents "huffed out."[17]

The sheer number and breadth of the library's programming is staggering. Beginning on September 23, lectures on Negro history took place every Wednesday evening. Covering ancient African history to the current Civil Rights Movement, the library had an impressive array of speakers including John Axam (director of the Philadelphia Free Library), Hassan Ishangi (Ishangi African Cultural Center), Judge Rainey (WDAS Radio Station), Jeremiah X (Nation of Islam mosque), and Prathia Hall (SNCC). An NSM report states how the library could use a permanent lecturer, one who could develop a Negro history reference section.[18]

Initially, the guest speakers and topics appealed to the local demographic Churchville hoped to target. Yet as time went on, more and more middle- and upper-class people began to attend, which drove out the local and intended audience.[19]

Another educational initiative of the library was its neighborhood tutorial program. Realizing the schools surrounding Ridge Avenue were deficient in every way, Churchville recruited a handful of high school students to help him. Canvassing the surrounding neighborhood, the tutors "rounded up 60 children from forty-seven different families." This is less alarming than it may appear. Churchville and his tutors not only contacted each child's parents for their permission but also obtained permission from each child's school. When it came to education, everyone needed to be on the same page.[20]

Aimed at the elementary- and junior-high-aged students, the "program itself involved tutoring the children in specific subjects; helping them with their homework assignments by making dictionaries, reference books and encyclopedias available to them; and showing them how to use these reference works." This was no easy task. Not only were the students academically behind their age groups, but also their respective home lives were not conducive to supporting any interest in education.[21]

In addition to the high school student tutors, gang members were also recruited to help teach. "Look, man, you only read at the fifth grade level," began Churchville's standard approach, "but you read more than this kid. So teach him what you know." Churchville also worked hard to position the library as a positive alternative to "counteract the negative social identities of the ghetto."[22]

To further meet the needs of the community, the library also offered a preschool program. Even though it was obvious some parents were only using it to get their children "out of their hair," the library itself took the program quite seriously. For one hour per day, toddlers could be exposed to "education objectives," "learning to see," and "developing creativity." This threefold objective consisted of "exercises, dances and puzzles . . . [drawing] pictures of themselves and surroundings," and "[making] things out of paper, clay and cloth."[23]

The arts were also well represented at the library. The Freedom Concert Choir hovered between twenty-five and forty members

Books seized by police in Black Muslim headquarters on West Columbia Avenue. Many of these items would find their way to the Freedom Library. *Courtesy of Temple University Libraries, Special Collections Research Center.*

who gave performances not only as fundraisers but also "to inspire understanding and appreciation of choral singing as a mode of personal and musical expression."[24]

Also meeting weekly was the Music Appreciation Club, which focused on "the Negro's development and use of the rhythm, blues, spiritual, and jazz idioms." The attendance of this club remains unknown, but someone did note that it also attended local concerts and visited some of Philadelphia's music schools. An art program was also provided, featuring instruction in sketching, lectures in art history, and trips to art galleries.[25]

A scan of the environment also saw two more programs added at the library. One was the Community Action Program, which sought to combat Philadelphia's inferior housing problem. A survey conducted by the library found a strong percentage of low-income families paying exorbitantly high rent in homes of low quality. After presenting its findings on a local radio, a three-tiered solution was created to have library volunteers advocate to the city on behalf of its residents.[26]

WHAT LIES BEYOND HATE

Gangs were also a reality of life in north Philadelphia, and the library sought to provide alternatives to the youth caught up in this lifestyle. In October of 1964, Churchville invited the leaders of three local gangs to meet with him at the library. Along with a handful of other teenagers, a discussion of job-preparedness and positive choices took place. A second meeting took place, and the Neighborhood Youth Program (soon changed to the Intra-City Community Cooperative, Inc.) was formed. "Combatting poverty" was the group's mission statement, which even earned them a field trip to Washington, DC.[27]

Similar to this was the library's Leadership Training Program, which targeted the "non-school or drop-out persons." This initiative hoped to help this group "search for ways that they, as part of the community, can be effective in shaping that environment to their own values."[28]

"In its first year of existence, the NSM Freedom Library has involved 250 people of varying ages in regular participation in our programs." This sentence opened a report noting how the library continued to operate on Ridge Avenue for a full year right into the summer of 1965. It also noted the successes of the varied programs. The Negro history lectures continued to meet once per week, with attendance "between 25 and 45 people." The Neighborhood Tutorial Program—now renamed the Afternoon Tutorial—was currently at "150 young people regularly participating." The preschool program had grown as well, as did the varied art and music programs.[29]

The two youth programs were still in existence, but their success remained questionable. The "extreme hostility and alienation" of gang members made community leadership and positive experiences difficult to sustain. And like every other library everywhere, "the only limits that have hindered us have been financial."[30]

And that is not entirely true. Other outside factors continued to interfere with the library's success. One was the assassination of Malcolm X by Nation of Islam members in February of 1965. Churchville "was devastated" at the news and hung Malcolm's photo back up in the library's window. Once again, he found Jeremiah X pacing nervously in his mother's home.[31]

Soon after that, Deborah Mills—a fourteen-year-old who tutored others in the afternoon programs—was badly beaten by police outside her home, causing her mother to suffer a heart attack. A neighbor drove them both to St. Joseph's Hospital, where they were denied admittance on the pretence of not having arrived in an ambulance.[32]

One of the worst events would take place a year later, on the evening of August 13, 1966. Just before one in the morning, eighty police in full riot gear, backed by one thousand uniformed officers, conducted raids on two apartments, an SNCC Center City office, and the NSW Freedom Library.[33]

Living upstairs above the library with his wife, Churchville found himself being shoved against a wall in his kitchen. Concerned for the safety and well-being of his wife, Churchville stated he was in full cooperation with them, and they could do what they had to do. One officer began to push Churchville quite forcefully (hoping to get him to "do something stupid"), while the others tore open the ceiling and overturned the apartment's cabinets and drawers. Then they left just as suddenly as they had arrived.[34]

The police claimed to be acting on the charge that the SNCC had been stockpiling dynamite and arms. The NSW Freedom Library had been seen as having ties to the SNCC, so it was raided as well. That the police "failed to find any dynamite or weaponry in their searches" provided little solace for Churchville and his wife. Sleeping became difficult, as every sound from the street triggered an expectation that the building's doors would be kicked in again.

"I was enraged," Churchville remembers. "How have I behaved in this neighborhood? I've never had a gun." He decided though to eventually let it go, realizing he was "getting off track from what I need to be doing to help people. . . . I sucked it up, basically, and I was wise to do so."[35]

The NSW Freedom Library continued as it had before. Similar to the Freedom Libraries before it, it attracted not only the community members it hoped to serve but also activists as well. Veering away from the integrationist efforts of the Civil Rights Movement, these activists were interested in "an all-black political organization." Under the auspices of the Freedom Library, they formed the Black People's Unity Movement (BPUM). This new organization would be "committed to black nationalist principles of racial unity, black consciousness, and community control."[36]

BLACK PEOPLE'S UNITY MOVEMENT

"Because the problem of Black People in America is not one of civil rights," read a document titled "Unity Program," "but is, and has always been, the domination of white supremist society, it is necessary to form a movement of Black People to fight against racism and secure to Black People their full human rights." Another document had "ONE PEOPLE—ONE NEED—ONE FIGHT" typed out apart from the main text, evidence of an accepted motto or one that needed to be tested.[37]

Churchville, who was the natural head of the BPUM, knew enough to want the new organization not to dissolve over philosophical differences. He ensured the group was welcoming of anyone's ideology—including his own. By the time the BPUM was created, Churchville had converted to Christianity, and he wanted the group to be governed by "Jesus' leadership principles." This didn't bode well for many. "Well," one brave soul asked Churchville directly, "how do we get rid of you?"[38]

The BPUM was also to be inclusive of all. Churchville envisioned it to include "gang members, old ladies, young people, professionals, people who were aspiring for politics—we wanted to have people who were musicians and dancers." By 1966, the BPUM had all these groups represented—this incredible stratum of socioeconomically diverse people belonging to it. All were welcomed.[39]

Unless you were white.

The minutes of the NSM Freedom Library's staff meeting dated October 8, 1965, confirms this racial stance. South African political activist Isaac Bangani Tabata was coming to speak at the Freedom Library later that month as part of the library's Black history program. "Whitey can attend the press conference," the minutes noted in a discussion of program logistics. "But not the History program."[40]

That white people were not allowed was not a secret; the library advertised it was open to "all Black People who are serious about Freedom." In its first month of operation, a group running out of Temple University challenged Churchville on this policy. "Here was an early attempt by the Philadelphia Tutorial Project (a project located at Temple University started by the NSM) to pressure us to take on white staff or volunteers. We didn't bite, so that was the end of that."[41]

A student reporter from the *Temple University News* pushed the director to explain himself further. Noting that the volunteers he was being asked to accommodate were middle-class white students, he felt "it would be difficult if not impossible" for these students to develop appropriate programs that were outside the middle-class, white viewpoint. They could never understand the "tremendous sense of worthlessness and self-hate" found in the library's target demographic.[42]

"Discrimination in reverse" was a charge laid by the *Philadelphia Tribune* in February of 1966, after a Georgia senate member and SNCC's communication director came to speak at a rally sponsored by the BPUM. The accusation came after reporters noticed that only African Americans were allowed to attend. A letter to the *Tribune*'s editor written the following day challenged this claim, stating that she—as a white woman accompanied by her white friends—had been allowed to attend. She also questioned why

"A BLACK UNITY RALLY" was not accepted by the paper, for it clearly is in its own title.[43]

"Recently I came upon a lady who alleged," began a brief write-up in the library's newsletter, "that we here at the FREEDOM LIBRARY hate white people." The author, a youth volunteer named Gary R. Adams, countered this: "Personally, I don't hate anyone." He then listed a series of violent hate crimes committed against African Americans by law enforcement that took place in Chester, Pennsylvania—the town he grew up in. He concluded with: "Isn't this enough to make anybody hate? Yes, but I don't hate the white folks who did these things (or Grizzly Bears) but I know them."[44]

All the complaints about discrimination appear to have been moot. There is no memory of anyone of any race other than African American even visiting the library, let alone attempting to use its collection or attend any of the programs. It is unknown if they would have been turned away outright, or if they would have been given access.[45]

As mentioned in chapter 5, the SNCC was going through the exact organizational growing pains mentioned above. Integration versus Black Nationalism had always been topics of debate in the organization, but by 1965 lines began to be drawn. "Black Power" began to be the driving force of the SNCC. "Marches, beatings, protests, murders, and counter-demonstrations began to suck the life out of the organization," Maria Varela remembers experiencing. By 1966, white members were asked to leave the SNCC. For the African Americans to obtain real freedom rights, "race-based strategies for black empowerment . . . came to be considered absolutely necessary."[46]

History now recognizes this divisive split as "false dichotomy"— there was much more going on than the obvious optics of this "is/ or" choice. "Nationalism and integrationist are inadequate terms to describe the vast range of political insights that have been outgrowths of past struggles."[47]

Incredibly, Churchville would run the Ridge Avenue Freedom Library until 1978, although it ceased being an actual library in 1967. Continued clashes with the Northern Student Movement and concern for the safety of his wife and future children caused

Churchville to "drop out of activist politics." Teaching was where his heart lay. He and his wife purchased the storefront outright and turned it into the Freedom Library Day School—one of the country's first Pan African nationalist classrooms.[48]

During the summer of 1965, Churchville received a letter from Michael Dei-Anang, the secretary for Ghana's president, Dr. Kwame Nkrumah. "Osagyefor The President . . . congratulates you on the establish of the Freedom Library, with its concern for promoting a positive identity of Afro-Americans with their home continent. . . . The President asks me to convey to you and your organization his best wishes for its continued success."[49]

FOR THOSE WHO HAVE NO THEATER

Black empowerment would also create an ideological shift in the Free Southern Theater (FST), resulting in a Freedom Library appearing in the Ninth District of New Orleans. Similar to the SNCC, the evolution to Black Power was politically and personally divisive among the FST performers and its board of directors. Lack of financial stability also moved the company from Jackson, Mississippi, to New Orleans, creating more hard feelings among those who felt FST was abandoning its original mission.

As mentioned in chapter 3, the FST was created to bring real theater into the southern states, which would bring "a form of cultural expression that spoke directly to black experience in the rural and urban south." Touring the places the SNCC had an established presence, the Free Southern Theater was the perfect complement to Freedom Library activity. Decades later the American Library Association would agree, stating, "Visual and performing arts can transform understanding and appreciation of the world in all its cultural diversity. The American Library Association affirms that visual and performing arts can be powerful components of library collections and services."[50]

Besides bringing "a theater for those who have no theater," the company is now recognized as "one of America's bravest theaters." Like all movement workers and volunteers, they withstood the daily terror of Jim Crow, with its "racist violence . . . fires, police raids, bomb threats [and] arrests." Most performers slept not in beds but under them, hoping to avoid being killed when locals began to blast away at the homes they were staying at. The FST soon found it necessary to perform under armed guard.[51]

There were surprises, though. A late performance at the Indianola Freedom Center was interrupted one night by an army of vehicles descending on it. People feared the worst as more than forty police in riot gear exited their cars and surrounded the place. "It looked like a very orderly lynching party," wrote a reporter from the *Nation*. Another two dozen people not in uniforms arrived lining up behind a man wearing a three-piece suit and a cowboy hat. Announcing himself as the local sheriff, he asked a question no one expected: "Can we see the play?"[52]

African Americans were not the only ones who had no experience with live theater, so everyone squeezed in until it was stand-

Denise Nicholas and the Free Southern Theater, Mileston, Mississippi, 1964. *Photo by Matt Herron. Courtesy of The Image Works.*

ing room only. Although the overcrowding caused temperatures to rise to 110 degrees, both races watched, laughed, and applauded as one. Although the reporter felt that no strides were made in race relations that evening, surely this was something.

Among the plays performed that year was Samuel Beckett's *Waiting for Godot,* which well-meaning outsiders felt was inappropriate for the African American community. This bias against *Godot* repeatedly surfaced, as some felt the play far too highbrow and complex for an audience made up of many uneducated and illiterate people. "What possible relevance," FST member Denise Nicholas was asked over and over, "do you imagine *Godot* to have to lives of black people in the South?"[53]

Evidently, a great deal. "Everyday we see men dressed just like these (tramps), sitting around the bars, pool halls, and on the street corners waiting for something. They must be waiting for Godot!" This was the voiced opinion of Ruleville's Fannie Lou Hamer, who—while possessing only a few years of elementary school education—grasped Beckett's theme of existential doom immediately. She stated she knew people who just sat around waiting for other people "to bring in Freedom," exactly like the men in the play. Again, the American Library Association would agree with Mrs. Hamer, stating, "The arts play a vital role in our ability to communicate a broad spectrum of ideas to all people."[54]

BOOKS IN THE GHETTO OF DESIRE

"There perhaps will be an increasing attempt on the part of black people to search out the facts of their history and culture; to study that literature which gives information regarding the basic sociological differences which exist in this century, such as the study and writings of W.E.B. Dubois, St. Clair Drake, Kenneth B. Clark, Richard Wright, etc."[55] This was the conclusion of a five-page report titled "The Preliminary Proposal for an Afro*American/ African Information Center," written by actress Denise Nicholas. Having visited numerous Freedom Libraries while touring with the Free Southern Theater (see chapter 3), she was familiar with their purpose and concept. Yet the idea for one did not hit until she was visiting another type of library: the New York Public.

Around Christmas of 1965, Nicholas was spending her time in the New York Public Library's Schomburg Center hunting down African plays that would be suitable for the Free Southern Theater to perform. She was distracted one day as another patron kept looking up at her from his book. Striking a conversation with him on one of her smoke breaks, she found out her admirer was a Muslim, and was researching "history from a black point of view." This struck Nicholas as something she and the rest of the Free Southern Theater had been grasping at, but never had the time to develop.[56]

Inspired, she exited the library and headed straight for Lewis Michaux's African National Bookstore on the corner of West 125th Street and 7th Avenue. After buying some works by Malcolm X and Franz Fanon, she was struck with an idea. "But more important than the books I bought that day, or any other day, I left that library feeling for the first time that something was beginning to glue black people back together again."[57]

"The first time I walked into the Schomburg Collection in Harlem," Nicholas wrote in an article for *Liberator*, "I knew we had to have some kind of public information center down here, with art objects done by Black people, photographs, films, slides, books, magazines, etc." She also wanted to replicate the liveliness of Freedom Libraries, and not one "like the Schomburg—quiet, firm, full of books that most of us don't read."[58]

Nicholas set up the Afro American/African Information Center at 1240 Dryades Street. This was "the most deprived black neighbourhood in New Orleans," "that filthy Ninth Ward," and "the center in New Orleans of every social ill." The flooded ruins of a supermarket in the Desire housing projects would be the best location for the library. Joseph K. Stevens, the FST technical director, built shelves for the library while Nicholas created a classification system.[59]

"I wanted to contribute," she would later write. "I wanted to see little children walk with their heads high, reading Negro history, understanding fully this bind Whitey put us in. . . . I began fathering small groups of youngsters in the hot early afternoon sun to read and look at pictures from Africa and other parts of the world." The combination of library and stage enabled the FST to offer outreach programs in acting, dance, creative writing, and black history.[60]

The Afro American/African Information Center did not last long. New Orleans held as much racial terror as Mississippi or Alabama, with Nicholas finding a policeman's gun jammed into her forehead one day as her fellow theater members were arrested for vagrancy. Combined to this was the internal strife the change of location and mission was having on long-time members. Nicholas could easily have weathered this if her calling was not clearly lying elsewhere. She left the FST in September of 1966, joining the Negro Ensemble Company in New York. From there she became an award-winning television and film actress, playwright, and novelist.

"Reverend Singleton's eyes shone in his brown face," Nicholas wrote in her novel *Freshwater Road*. "Like the idea of a library was the finest thing he'd ever heard."[61]

Chapter Seven

———————◯———————

Arkansas
We Are All Connected

"Say 'elevator.'"

In the close of Sanderia Faye's autobiographical novel *Mourner's Bench,* ten-year-old Sarah Jones has become infuriated with the civil rights worker who ran the Gould, Arkansas, Freedom Center Library. Having trouble pronouncing the letter *r,* young Sarah was asked to practice the word *elevator.* "Why?" she demanded to know. "Why in God's name would I ever have to say that word? We ain't got none in this town. I ain't never seen one and probably never will, so why, out of all the words we know, would you want me to say that one?"[1]

This scene had played out in Faye's real life—not about the word *elevator*—but about having to learn French. Classes in French were offered in the summer of 1965 at the Gould Freedom Center Library. These classes were presented by Laura Foner, a New Yorker and recent graduate of Brandeis University. Foner turned down a scholarship to Harvard to volunteer in Arkansas. Racial terror hung over everything in the state, as Foner soon discovered when Gould's chief of police told her that if she didn't go back north, he would cut her head off.[2]

Fictional Jones and actual Faye were correct about questioning the use of the word *elevator* and the French language. The intergenerational fears caused by white supremacy produced a pervasive hopelessness in the African Americans of Arkansas. There is very little concept of a future life when your people are seen collectively as nothing, and you are seen individually as nobody.

Changing this was the raison d'être of the Gould Freedom Center Library, despite being housed in a building that looked like it would collapse at any moment. With the help of locals, Foner arranged furniture, built shelves, and unpacked and arranged the books that had been donated. Not only had the children of Gould never seen a new book before, but they had also never seen any written by African Americans. Foner also set up a mini classroom, announcing she would be teaching classes in "black history, government, and French."[3]

French! The young Faye thought Foner was crazy. If the word *elevator* was a huge waste of time, learning a foreign language was next to useless. "Why on earth would I have to learn French?"

BEGINNINGS

Arkansas needed help.

The state itself was a bundle of contradictions during the Civil Rights Movement. Although *Brown v. Board of Education* had played itself out in the city of Little Rock in the late 1950s, school integration had not followed in any logical or peaceful way. The state also had a higher standard of living and burgeoning middle class, yet "endemic poverty" marked most communities. Arkansas was also seen as a more tolerant, progressive, and less violent state—one in which parents would be more comfortable sending their children to school, compared to, say, Alabama or Mississippi. This simply turned out not to be true. Arkansas experienced as much "hard core racism" as any other southern state, complete with mass arrests and horrific violence.[4]

The racial barriers were also blurred, resulting in puzzling behaviors. The African American community was inconsistent at best during this time, with some actively resisting any civil rights activity, including an NAACP president engaging in voter fraud to elect a white official. The president of Arkansas Agricultural, Mechanical & Normal College also acted erratically. After telling students he would not expel them if they chose to demonstrate, he did just that.

Hanging over everything was the Elaine Massacre—a bloody race riot "in which an estimated 200-plus African Americans were killed, another 285 were arrested and 12 men were sentenced to death." African Americans lived under the shadow of the incident for decades after, being reminded indirectly—and often directly— of the consequences for challenging the state's hold on white supremacy.[5]

The desegregation of Central High School in Little Rock also overshadowed daily life in Arkansas. The ruling of *Brown v. Board of Education* stated segregating public schools to be unconstitutional, but translating this ruling into reality would turn out to be "human torture" for the children chosen for this task.

Melba Pattillo Beals had just turned twelve when the May 17, 1954, ruling of *Brown* was announced. Her junior high school teacher announced it, and then sent all of her students home for the day. "Pay attention to where you are walking," her teacher instructed the dismissed students. "Walk in groups, don't walk alone. . . . Hurry." Beals did not listen to her teacher and began to daydream while walking home alone. She was badly beaten and sexually assaulted by a large man who screamed at her about "niggers wanting to school with his children."[6]

As part of the Little Rock Nine, attending the all-white school was no better for her. Fellow students punched and kicked her daily, and one even poured acid into her eyes. Her heels were stomped on and kicked so frequently she had difficulty walking in her adult years. Although she and her fellow students finished the school year, the Arkansas governor closed the school for the entirety of the following year. The amassing of white supremacy, states' rights, federal troops, and closed schools may have appeared to increase racial tension in Arkansas, but in reality, these events only highlighted what had been there all along.[7]

Nat Griswold was doing everything he could to ensure freedom rights for African Americans, but was not having much luck. A Methodist minister from Little Rock, Griswold was the executive director of the Arkansas Council on Human Relations since its founding in 1954. "A long record of failures" was how Griswold characterized his organization's work. After the Central High efforts blew up, the ACHR found its efforts to be hindered sometimes directly, but more by apathy. Without any organized and ongoing direct pressure, Arkansas communities would continue to cling to their Jim Crow way of life.[8]

Arkansas was in trouble. Realizing outside help was needed, Griswold placed a long-distance phone call to Atlanta, Georgia, and the offices of the SNCC. A Western Union telegram addressed to Revered Nat Griswold arrived at his office on October 23, 1962. It read "Bill Hansen, Field Secretary for the Student Nonviolent Coordinating Committee will arrive Little Rock tomorrow afternoon. He will call office on arrival. Best Wishes."[9]

The telegram came from Dorothy Miller, the communications director for the SNCC. Under the direction of Bill Hansen, the SNCC would conduct sit-ins and protests, voter registration, and of course books and library service via community freedom houses.

RUBBING SHOULDERS WITH COLORED PEOPLE

Library services for African Americans in Arkansas followed exactly that of other southern states—nonexistent or the inferior segregated type. A telling example occurred in 1906, when the city of Little Rock petitioned Andrew Carnegie to fund the construction of a whites' only public library. Not only was this perfectly fine, but also Carnegie's own assistant was worried that news of his boss having dinner with Booker T. Washington would be offensive to Little Rock's civic leadership. On the contrary, was one leader's reply. Not only did he have fond childhood memories of his father bringing a preferred slave to dinner, but also "it was his white right to [choose] the colored people he sat at dinner with or rubbed shoulders with at the library."

An odd statement from someone who had no intention of rubbing shoulders with any African American, let alone permit them to enter Little Rock's public library.[10]

By mid-century, Arkansas boasted only two segregated libraries against the state's one hundred. Small efforts were being made during this time. African Americans using the public library in Magnolia were permitted to check out books from a collection donated by other African Americans, and only at a separate desk with a separate African American staff member. Pine Bluff was a bit more progressive, allowing its users to check out a book from the main branch if the segregated branch did not have it. Six years before the crisis at their Central High School, the town of Little Rock allowed African American college students access to the town's public library.[11]

The importance of books and reading was evident in the African American community even against all the racial restrictions.

Terrence Roberts—who along with Beal was one of the Little Rock Nine—remembers a "shared love of reading" in his home. "We read everything we could find," Roberts recollected, "repeatedly combing the shelves of the Ivy Branch library, the public library for black people, to find books that may have somehow escaped our attention during earlier visits." While his parents hoped use of the segregated library would help Roberts and his siblings "reach beyond the ordinary," there was still an emotional cost to using it, one still felt fifty years later.[12]

"In Little Rock as a young person I wondered often about the rationale for a system that did not allow black kids to have access to the bigger libraries in town. The very small Ivy Branch was obviously designed to underscore the point that we were not seen as worthy of having greater access to all that libraries have to offer."[13]

Gertrude Jackson's experience is also telling. Having moved from Illinois to Arkansas as a young girl, Jackson recalls how the school experience was "just so different." She went from a large elementary school with separate rooms for each grade, with each room having its own "little room where you hang your coats and things," to having to walk four miles to the one-room schoolhouse that ended at the eighth grade. "Nigger, nigger, nigger" was frequently yelled at her by Marvell's white neighbors being bused to their own school.[14]

Outside the Gould Freedom Center. *Photo by Laura Foner.*

Her own children would attend that same school in the early 1960s; sporadically it would often flood with sewage, which made the room and its drinking water unfit.

One her most painful memories was when one of her daughters came home and said she wished she had been born white. When asked why, her daughter replied, "So we can have some swings and some seesaws and have a pretty school." One can only imagine the pain of watching one's children go to a school that not only resembled the sewer but also had no playground to encourage relaxation, physical health, and well-being. "Just the naked ground," Jackson remembers. "Just nothing."[15]

Access to books was equally important to Melba Pattillo Beals as well. The Little Rock Public Library was off limits to her, and the libraries in her elementary and junior high school were terribly small and of course not very good. One saving grace was her mother, who worked at the Baptist College Library. Every few weeks she and her brother were allowed to go with her mother to work and take out books. Although not as big as the public library, it was well stocked with all kinds of books. While the staff and students were primarily African American, some at the Baptist College were white, which made Beals and her brother apprehensive.[16]

Bill Hansen arrived in the town of Little Rock shortly on the heels of the telegram that preceded him. Born and raised in Cincinnati, Hansen had dropped out of Xavier University so he could dedicate all his time to the Civil Rights Movement. He was just twenty-one when he arrived in Little Rock, still nursing broken ribs with his jaw wired shut, the result of being arrested for protesting in Albany.

Five years had passed since the Central High Crisis, and Little Rock's white community leaders did not want a repeat of it. A "secret committee" had been formed by local business leaders, hoping African American freedom rights could be granted—or at least negotiated—secretly and behind closed doors. The city no longer wanted to be ground zero for the "US's racial shame."[17]

Hansen believed Griswold's request to the SNCC was to have an outside group absorb any racial hate and resentment. "That's the reason they called SNCC in the first place . . . because they were too afraid for their reputations and their nice suburban lifestyles. 'Call SNCC and have them take the heat. They'll do what we're afraid to do and then we'll step in later as the voice of reason and moderation and take the credit.' And that's exactly what they did."[18]

MORE BOOKS: MORE EXPERTISE

Hansen quickly organized volunteers not only in Little Rock, but also in Pine Bluff, Helena, and Gould. With Hansen directing nonviolent sit-ins and selective-buying tactics, a number of businesses and public places began to desegregate, albeit as quietly as possible. Each town had its own unique successes and failures. While two students were able to "peacefully integrate the Helena Public Library," the same two failed to do so at the city's swimming pool. Both were arrested and savagely beaten while in police custody.[19]

Learning from events in Mississippi and Alabama, the Arkansas SNCC would launch its own Freedom Summer in 1965. Although the Civil Rights Act had been signed into legislation the previous year, and the Voting Rights Act was quickly coming, Arkansans were still deprived of their constitutional rights. The goals of the Arkansas Summer Project were "to combat segregation in public facilities and schools, to assist in voter registration, and to raise the consciousness of black citizens."[20]

Although the number of incoming northern students and volunteers was quite small compared to other states, the books and experience were not. Bill Hansen recalls that "based upon the Mississippi experience the previous summer, we tended to have more books and a greater expertise with [freedom] schools and libraries."[21]

Freedom Libraries were established in Gould, Helena, and Forrest City. These cities had "more of a library sense; more books, more emphasis on their availability. SNCC had two kinds of facilities: living quarters and offices/community hangouts. Quite often both were one physical location." Hansen also recalls sometimes centers were only "sometimey"—opening and suddenly closing whenever staff and money ran out. Even with these, though, "there was always a bookshelf. There were always books."[22]

A Freedom House had actually been in operation in Helena since the previous summer, but at a great cost. Being in the SNCC office was a terrifying ordeal for the workers. Sleep was impossible, as white supremacists spent each night driving around the house and yelling threats. One night a mob numbering 150 descended on it, causing the workers to run out the back and hide in an adjoining field. Homes allowing SNCC workers to stay with them were shot up and firebombed. Historian Grif Stockley wrote, "In retrospect, it is amazing no SNCC workers were killed."[23]

Although an inventory of the Helena Freedom House listed "two cars, two typewriters, and one mimeograph machine," no record of book titles or number of books has survived. There is also no record or memory of the type of library activity that occurred there. In general, all Freedom Houses in Arkansas planned to "provide recreational and educational opportunities for children and teenagers," with topics including "African Culture, Negro History [and] Current Events."[24]

Forrest City shared a similar fate. Bill Hansen remembers it being located in an "old, abandoned funeral home with all kinds of rooms; classes, libraries, offices, etc." Known as the Forrest City Freedom Center, the building boasted eleven rooms. What is known is that "two local teachers and two SNCC activists worked with from fifteen to thirty students twice daily." Hansen recalls of both places that "there were always books and there were always people borrowing them."[25]

The Freedom House in Gould was different. Housed in a building owned by a local woman, not only did it have one of the larger book collections, but it also had a future librarian.

THE CHILDREN'S LIBRARIAN

Born and raised in New York, Laura Foner had been interested in helping secure freedom rights since she could remember. Suspected of communist leanings, her father Philip had been fired from his teaching job at New York City College during the McCarthy era, which impacted her greatly. She belonged to an NAACP youth group while in high school and became involved with the Friends of SNCC while attending Brandeis University. It was through this connection she heard of the Arkansas Summer Project, to which she applied and was accepted.

Her arrival in Gould was both welcomed and resented. An African American from Mississippi had been helping organize things in Gould, and—in addition to his thinly disguised hatred of white people—he felt her presence would only "inflame the white population and escalate an already tense situation." Out of genuine concern for her safety as well, it was decided that Foner would work at the Freedom House only, and not out in the field.[26]

The building itself resembled those in other states, an abandoned and decrepit structure; "cardboard boxes covered broken windows, cracks in the walls let cold winter air in, and the bathroom fixtures needed repair." The house was owned by Carrie

Laura Foner teaching African American history at the Gould Freedom
Center Library. *Courtesy of Laura Foner.*

Dilworth, one senior citizen who welcomed the SNCC not only
into Gould but also into her home. Foner lived with her for almost
a year, remembering Dilworth as a "mentor, protector, and friend."
The long-time Gould resident had been fearlessly organizing protests since the 1930s, and it appeared there was no stopping her in
her golden years. While Foner was adjusting to her new residence,
Dilworth descended on Little Rock's federal courthouse, demanding something be done about Gould's high school library, which had
only thirty books of little or no use in a crumbling building.[27]

Foner spent the summer of 1965 converting the two-story Freedom Center with the help of three other SNCC volunteers. One
room was designated a classroom, one room a large boardroom for
meetings, and one for the library. As the volunteers helped build
shelves, Foner began to unpack and arrange a very special collection

of books. The Friends of SNCC had donated 1,500 books. Most were new. All were about African American history. As mentioned above, many citizens of Gould had never seen a new book before.

"I didn't know what I was doing," Foner recalls, "setting up a library with classes and programs and activities for kids." Fortunately, the SNCC had provided her with a basic curriculum that had been used in Mississippi the previous summer. "There was basic literacy, and black histories and simple lessons. But I had no idea what I was doing. I was so young."[28]

Foner didn't have much to do with collection development, as the books had already been chosen by others and shipped to her. "The kids were excited," she recalls. "It was thrilling for them to have books that were new. Most of them did not have any books in their house except maybe a Bible. And their school books were the old raggedy used kind that were passed down from the white

Gould Freedom Center Library. *Courtesy of Gould Freedom Center Library.*

school." The Freedom House Library would change all this. "Many had never seen books by black authors; about their own history; their own culture."[29]

One book that was a big hit was *A Pictorial History of the Negro in America* by Langston Hughes and Milton Meltzer. It was actually a book that had been in Foner's own home when she was growing up. "It was a great big book with a lot of wonderful photographs. The children just loved it."[30]

Other popular books were Richard Wright's *Black Boy*, Peter Judd's *African Independence*, and an anthology titled *Three Negro Classics*, which included W. E. B. Du Bois's *The Souls of Black Folk*, *The Autobiography of a Colored Man* by James Weldon Johnson, and Booker T. Washington's *Up from Slavery*.[31]

Negroes in American History: A Freedom Primer was also very much in demand. "[It] is a history book about us," one student stated, possibly accounting for its popularity. "It is about a history that has been denied us by lies about what we are and what we have been."[32]

EVERYBODY CAN USE IT

The library itself was important to the children, and the children "were the really important part of the movement. A very important part." Besides being able to borrow books and take classes, there was a lot of recreational activity as well. Singing, board games, and even basketball games took place. "The girls taught me jump rope and dances," Foner recalls.[33]

They also taught her a lot about living in a society that views you as less than human. One of her more distressing memories was being shown the segregated high school. "It consisted of four wooden buildings that were totally falling apart. There was no running water, no indoor plumbing, holes in the building, holes in the walls. The books were tattered. These four buildings were called Jap Huts," because they were leftover shacks that had been used to incarcerate Japanese people during the Second World War. "It set off explosions in my mind," Foner recalls. "We are all connected."[34]

The SNCC workers and local people were also the target of Klan threats, unlawful police raids and intimidation, as well as the general anger and resentment felt by "all the whites." As mentioned above, Foner recalls a large number of African Americans resenting their presence as well. "They saw us as troublemakers and wished we would go away."[35]

"One of the things we do in libraries is we encourage children to share their story and to hear the stories of all kinds of people from all over the world." This practice also took place in Gould, when students would drop by after school. They would tell Foner and others of the horrors they were experiencing at the white school—similar to what Beals experienced in Little Rock (see above).[36]

Eight years after the Little Rock Crisis, Gould was only now integrating their schools. In hopes of stonewalling reality, Gould would permit African Americans to enroll in two grades only. As

Gould Freedom Center Library. *Courtesy of Laura Foner.*

the first day of classes rolled around, Foner accompanied a large group of parents and their children to try and admit all the students into all the grades. At the refusal of school officials to admit anyone except for those in the specific two grades, Foner and others spent the day protesting outside the school (picket signs, songs, and chanting). Threats were made on this group by other parents, onlookers, Klan members, and even law enforcement. While Foner was not arrested, the sheriff marched her into the back of his patrol car, promising to "chop her head off and throw it in the river."[37]

After a long season of local police depriving citizens of the right to protest, unlawful home invasions, and unwarranted arrests, along with voter fraud and practices of school officials, the SNCC requested and demanded federal assistance. The FBI, having an increased presence in the state since the Central High Crisis, began to interview the complainants and victims. Foner was one of the first to be interviewed, having received a direct threat of murder from the sheriff.

"Someone from a local (not sure where) FBI office came to see me in Gould after I was threatened," Foner recalls. "I don't remember whether they mentioned my father, but they did not seem very concerned about my safety or the safety of the citizens of Gould."[38]

Whether mentioning Foner's father to her or not, the FBI was indeed only concerned with Foner because of her father. Although he lost his job and was blacklisted (see above), Philip Foner still became a respected U.S. historian and prolific author. Still obsessed with the red menace, the FBI instructed its Arkansas agents to "monitor the younger Foner since her father had spoken at a Fair Play for Cuba rally in New York City in November 1963 and taught at the New York School for Marxist Studies."[39]

Her father was also the author of *Frederick Douglass: A Biography*—one of the most requested books for Freedom Libraries in all southern states.

With Foner's encouragement, a preteen named Brenda Everett wrote down what the library meant to her. It appeared in a mimeographed newsletter titled *The Gould Freedom News*. "The Freedom Library," Everett's work began, "is in better condition than the school of Gould Arkansas." She continued: "Some people come to the Freedom Center and some don't but really it is a really handy place, especially the library it has book about negro History, children book, mazines, novels, encolpeida, Reader disgests, French book, game book, Science book, Work book, Play book and Family book. The library is open everyday and everybody can use it."[40]

In addition to a fairly sophisticated review of James Baldwin's *Blues for Mister Charlie,* she recommends a book on how to learn French. If more of her peers learned French, they would all "learn something that white people don't know, [and] that Gould can learn something there already making progress to more by the day."[41]

Freedom Centers with libraries were also established in the communities north of Gould, including Pine Bluff, Forrest City, and West Helena.

"I began to think we don't need to be doing this," Myrtle Glascoe recalls thinking. "Because the hostility was so tremendous and there was great anger." A social worker from California,

Children's librarian Laura Foner helping one of her "after-school regulars" at the library, 2014. *Courtesy of Laura Foner.*

Glascoe was the director of the West Helena Freedom Center. Older than most SNCC volunteers, Glascoe possessed a graduate degree in social work, as well as extensive experience working with at-risk youth with debilitating mental and emotional conditions.[42]

Originally disagreeing with nonviolent tactics and direct action, she eventually joined the Friends of SNCC in California before departing to Arkansas, where she was a "natural fit" as director of the West Helena Freedom Center, where she focused on providing books and classes. While her focus was mostly on teaching, she was passionate about the center's collection. "Books by Negroes, about Negroes" would be her focus.[43]

Nine volunteers worked out of West Helena. Glascoe was only one of two African Americans; she recalls wondering if this ratio was suitable enough to serve the community.

FUNERAL ARRANGEMENTS

In Forrest City, an SNCC volunteer named Millard Lowe hung a photo in the funeral home/freedom house. The image was of a public drinking fountain with a "whites only" sign hung over it. Lowe was asking the young people who had gathered before him if they could guess as to where exactly this photo was taken. Right here in Arkansas was the first guess, followed by Mississippi and Alabama. "This is in South Africa where it says 'whites only' by the water fountains as well." Lowe was trying to drive home the point that what was going on in Forrest City was also happening globally. "We were all in this whole thing together, this worldwide struggle."[44]

Lowe taught a course about Africa at the Freedom Center, connecting the American freedom struggle with others halfway around the world. Two books by Ghanaian president Kwame Nkrumah—his autobiography titled *Ghana*, and *Africa Must Unite*—were used as an instructional text with copies available in the library, sitting on the shelves that used to hold embalming fluid.

A native Texan, Lowe was studying education at Texas Southern University when he attended an SNCC rally and immediately signed on and was assigned to Forrest City. After stumbling over his first name—"Millard" (it sounded like people were saying "My Lord")—Lowe was assigned the nickname "Tex" (by who else, Stokely Carmichael).[45]

Florence Kathryn Clay had run the Clay Funeral Home with her husband until his death in 1957. She then took over as sole director, and offered her business to the SNCC while she and her brother were constructing a new one a few blocks away. "Mrs. Clay," as she was known to everyone, also opened her home as a place for Lowe to stay. Both these moves increased police harassment of both Lowe and the Clay family.[46]

More than once the Arkansas State Troopers would conduct raids on the Freedom House. "Arkansas finest . . . came for us one night in the old funeral home, and we had to hide," Lowe remembered. "And there was no place for us to hide but in those caskets. I never knew a casket was aeriated . . . they're soft and they're cushioned. I know this because I am still alive. We closed the tops, and we are in there for about, I don't know—maybe it was five, ten, fifteen, thirty minutes, one hour, three hours. But the one thing I remember was that I could breathe. I never know to this day why they make coffins aeriated."[47]

Between hiding from the police raids and mass arrests, Lowe focused on teaching what he could out of the Freedom House library. "In the library I taught weekly classes in African History, Caribbean History and African American History, which was called 'Ourstory.'"[48]

In the fall, the Forrest City School District faced a mass boycott of African American students, signaling their and their parents' utter frustration with the insincere gestures of limited integration. The state police arrested over two hundred students and SNCC workers, including Lowe. Nightly vigils were held outside the overflowing jail, while parents were told all charges would be dropped "if they signed documents promising to keep their children away from SNCC's Freedom Center and out of future demonstrations." As neither side refused to budge, Lowe discovered he was to be made an example of. He was charged with "some draconian law that would have kept him in jail into the next decade if he was convicted," and transferred to a prison in Mississippi where he was brutally beaten.[49]

GROWING PAINS

As 1965 moved into 1966, things outside the state were moving quickly. With passage of both the Civil Rights Act of 1964 and the Voting Rights Act of 1965, what history now calls the heroic period of the Civil Rights Movement had come to a close. The racial barriers that prevented African Americans from participating fully in American life were removed as a point of law.

The movement in Arkansas began to change drastically as well, and not because the heroic era had closed. A change in leadership and philosophy of the SNCC at the national level created repercussions felt immediately in Arkansas. The strategic practice of nonviolent protest was no longer welcomed in the organization; neither were white people. By the time these changes made their way into places like Gould and West Helena, it no longer mattered. While the SNCC-sponsored Freedom Libraries began to dissolve, the SNCC itself began to dissolve as well. The organization as a whole "collapsed under its own weight."[50]

This new phase was given a name in June of 1966. Fed up with being arrested for the twenty-seventh time in Mississippi, Stokely Carmichael told a large crowd that the time had come for "Black Power." With these two words, Carmichael "instantly transformed the aesthetics of the black freedom struggle and forever altered the course of the modern civil rights movement." The heroic phase of the movement had come to a close.[51]

Leaving Arkansas was extremely painful for all those involved. Foner recalls feeling "guilty and very sad leaving the people I had come to care about so much and who had welcomed me into their lives." Leaving the same month as Carmichael's speech, Foner relocated in Wisconsin to protest the Vietnam War. Months later the Gould Freedom Center was firebombed by the Arkansas Klan.[52]

Involved in various labor and women's movements, Foner eventually became a much-beloved children's librarian. "I remember applying to library school, and one of the application questions was whether you had ever worked in a library before. Which I hadn't. I had done many things, but I had never worked in a library. So I am trying to formulate into words why I wanted to be a librarian, and somewhere along the line it dawned on me that I had set up the Freedom School and the Freedom Library. So I put that in my application."[53]

Foner became the children's librarian at the Hyde Park Branch in Jamaica Plain, Massachusetts. She retired in 2014 and is remembered as "a mentor and a role model" by the library staff. "Her contributions to our community and to our children are invaluable."[54]

It could not have been easy for Bill Hansen to leave Arkansas either. Not only had he directed all the SNCC projects in Arkansas, but he had also married an activist from Pine Bluff. With a child on the way, Hansen needed to earn a living, and with no more SNCC funds available, he relocated to Atlanta and organized against rural poverty. Today he is Dr. Hansen, a professor and chair of international politics at the American University in Nigeria.

Millard Lowe returned to Texas to finish his education degree, and then relocated to Jamaica. He currently lives in Virginia, where, although retired, he still teaches. He also has numerous volumes of poetry published, and is highly involved in international literary scenes.

"Why on earth would I have to learn French?" the young Sanderia Faye asked Laura Foner at the Gould Freedom Library. "Because," replied Foner, kneeling down beside her, "because Sanderia, one day you are going to visit Paris."[55]

This was it right here—this was the reason for all the Freedom Libraries, if not the Civil Rights Movement itself. One single sentence had the power to cut through all the white hatred and injustice of the southern caste system. A young girl's limiting circumstances began to shift.

"Sanderia was a kid who came to the Freedom Center. She was there all the time. She told me [years later] that stuck in her head. And that she did visit Paris. She said at the time it was something that would never have occurred to her, or any of the students. It was like saying you are going to visit the moon. . . . She has written a novel—*Mourner's Bench*. It is really quite amazing."[56]

Foner isn't the only one who thinks that. *Mourner's Bench* won the Hurston/Wright Foundation Legacy Award in 2016, and both the Philosophical Society of Texas Book Award and the Arkansas

Library Association Arkansiana Award in 2017. Real-life Carrie Dilworth is part of the novel—opening her home up to house the SNCC Freedom Library. A volunteer from Georgia named Rutherford is determined to get a library card from the white segregated library, regardless of how many times he is arrested and beaten by police.

Not only did Faye become a novelist, but she is also a professor at Texas State University. She organizes various literary events in the South and is the co-founder of the Kimbilio Writer's Retreat.

"It was really significant we had shelves and books," Foner recalls about her time in Gould. "It meant a lot to the people there." There is no better statement that captures the people and events celebrated in this book. Fifty years later, there is no better statement for libraries anywhere.[57]

Chapter Eight

---◯---

Aftermath
The Long Dream

"I MOVED OVER TO THE BOOKSHELVES. I wanted to touch the books, but held back. Perhaps it is not permitted. Typed slips showed what each shelf held: novels, history, sociology, travel, Africana, political science, American Negro literature. . . . I stopped there. American Negro literature."

This was author Peter Abrahams's first experience at a library. The first book he reached for and opened was *The Souls of Black Folk* by W. E. B. Du Bois. Skimming a page, his brain swirled with memories as he read the phrase "the Negro is not free." He thought about the "whites only" signs he saw his entire life. "I remember the long walks in the white sections of the city, and the lavatories, and the park benches. . . . I remember spittle on my face."

Access to Du Bois's work caused Abrahams to have a life-altering epiphany: "'The Negro is not Free.' But why I had not thought of it myself? Now having read the words, I knew that I had known this all along. But until now I had had no words to voice that knowledge." As he read Du Bois's most famous line—"The problem of the Twentieth Century is the problem of the colour-line"—Abrahams knew something had changed within. "Du Bois had given me a key to the understanding of my world."[1]

The impact of this is slightly heightened when one knows this was written before the Civil Rights Movement, in London, by a

South African who had never set foot on American soil. Abrahams—exiled from his country during apartheid—had the above experience in Johannesburg's Bantu Men's Social Centre. The first of its kind opened to "Blacks," it consisted of one bookshelf holding two hundred books. The majority of these were by African American authors, many stemming from the Harlem Renaissance period. Other titles Abrahams would have had access to were *Up from Slavery* by Booker T. Washington, *Not without Laughter* by James Langston Hughes, The *Autobiography of an Ex-Colored Man* by James Weldon Johnson, and *Color* by Countee Cullen. A Freedom Library in every sense, it made at least one reader feel like he belonged among the African Americans discussed in this book. Why he felt so is obvious: human dignity recognizes itself in others.[2]

In the end, this was the mission of the Freedom Libraries, the mission of the Civil Rights Movement itself.

The American Civil Rights Movement remains "one of the defining events in American history," "one of America's greatest revolutions," and "the best, brightest, and most powerful display of democratic social change ever seen in the history of the United States." Or—more fittingly—as library historian Casper Leroy Jordan stated, it was the most important domestic movement that "profoundly changed both the economical and political scenes in America." He found "few events comparable" and "none more important."[3]

Half a century later, the Civil Rights Movement is as important and relevant today as it was back then. The history of the American Public Library is widely seen as a microcosm of America itself, and the Freedom Libraries were very much the embodiment of the Civil Rights Movement. Of course, not everyone agrees with this. In his influential work *The Last Days of Jim Crow in Southern Libraries*, Stephen Creswell states, "It is hard to escape the conclusion that efforts lavished on the freedom libraries were efforts misspent." Other scholars have supported this, believing that "Freedom Libraries alone did not change attitudes," or that "the question of library integration was never a major focus in the civil rights movement in the south."[4]

While it may have appeared that way to some, the people and events celebrated in the preceding chapters clearly illustrate that the Freedom Libraries had—and continue to have—a profound impact. They did so at the time of the Civil Rights Movement, and they continue to have a deep and meaningful influence on librarianship today. Their impact can be felt in the following ways:

- That accepted conditions needed for the existence of public libraries weren't necessary. A stable tax base, economic prosperity, and political stability have all been seen as necessary prerequisites for the existence and growth of a library in a given population. A literate population is also believed to be an essential condition. None of this was true of Freedom Libraries. In fact, most of them existed in communities that were openly hostile to them, in impoverished communities with a high illiteracy rate. They were also part of a movement that existed in stark contrast to both the political and social status quo.
- The importance of needs analysis. Sometimes referred to as environmental scanning or information audit, this is the process of a library's attempt at "understanding the potential and actual users of their services and collections." While it may have appeared obvious on what to provide a population whose library experience ranged from poor to none, imposing value judgments on the needs of a library's service community typically leads to erroneous choices. The Freedom Libraries were no exception to this. The Schwerners spent weeks going in and out of the community in order to create programs that would be of use to their patrons (see chapter 4).[5]
- The importance of collection management. Again, the nature of the Freedom Libraries should have made material selection an easier task than for most public libraries. Yet most were sent some odd choices, including books on Esperanto, numerous volumes of the Smithsonian Institution's financial reports, gossip magazines from Paris, seriously outdated textbooks, and women's fashion magazines from the Civil War era. "People's charitable throw-outs" were not in the best interest of the Freedom Libraries, a situation that remains today with modern libraries. While Freedom Library staff and volunteers knew instinctively what was of value to their patrons, today's libraries should have a proper

gift/donation policy in place to handle the well-intentioned but misguided contributions.[6]

- How to make do with less. Shrinking budgets and cutbacks result in today's libraries having "fewer employees, shorter hours, diminished collection budgets, [and] reduced programs and services." Although librarians are usually expert at creatively "making do" when funding is slashed, the profession should look to the Freedom Libraries, who did so much with so little. Both the SNCC and similar organizations paid their staff, but as more time went on, less money became available. After paying a building's rent, there was very little money left to put into collections or supplies. Somehow, adult, teen, and children's programming continued to grow, and some of the libraries had better holdings than comparable government-funded ones. The Freedom Libraries also engaged in community outreach, youth field trips, literacy classes, voter registration, and music appreciation.[7]

- A trained librarian makes all the difference. In no way should this downplay the work done by numerous workers and volunteers, many who quit their education, careers, and family ties, facing violence and sometimes murder. Without them, no Freedom Library would have been possible. There was a certain edge to those who had postsecondary education. They were familiar with how libraries worked: classification systems, borrowing procedures, and information-seeking behaviors. Virginia Steele—the only professionally trained librarian working in a Freedom Library at the time—brought so much more. She could recommend books and instruct others in cataloging techniques, book repair, and children's literacy. She arranged clipping files, craft supplies, adapting cataloging practices to suit local needs, all while coordinating and visiting all the other Freedom Libraries in Mississippi. She also insisted on giving each and every user a library card, knowing full well how important it could be to building self-esteem and a sense of belonging.

- A library is not a collection of books. Nor is it a building. Nothing proves these statements better than the firebomb destruction of the McComb Freedom House. With the building still smoldering, the afterschool youth just waited on the ground outside.

The children somehow knew what many adults in the twenty-first century have difficulty grasping: the fact that a library is a service, not a collection. A library exists for the librarians and patrons, not the other way around. In his 2014 TED Talk, Charlie Bennett stated that libraries "are a promise made by a community." Freedom Libraries remain the best illustration of this.[8]

- Libraries do indeed change lives. From Martin Luther King Jr. to the people mentioned throughout this book you may never have heard of, to you and me, free access to libraries changes who we are inside.

- Beacons of hope. Jim Crow was America at its worst. Public Libraries are America at its best. Bridging these two were the Freedom Libraries, which revealed the nightmare of library service in a segregated society, therefore aiding "a democracy aspiring to complete itself." Today, American libraries "serve as a powerful cultural symbol and visible goal for all democratic societies." Fifty years ago this was not the case, when skin color determined which citizen could participate in the democratic process. The Freedom Libraries helped stretch the limits of what was thought possible by people of any color.[9]

- Profiles of courage. Think about those who worked in the Freedom Libraries. Each faced administrative difficulties much more profound than budget cuts or staffing issues. They worked in an environment of hostile stakeholders, where physical harm was a daily reality. Many worked alone, making extraordinarily difficult choices, knowing that the fate of many depended on them. When today's circumstances appear untenable, library staff at all levels should take note of the powerful legacy left by the people who remain the embodiment of courage.

- Change is hard. The Freedom Libraries were agents of social change, standing hard against traditions and laws that were morally wrong and humanely indefensible. Perfectly capable of demanding racially segregated communities to change, many staff and volunteers felt confused, angry, and betrayed when the SNCC rapidly changed its mission from creating an integrated society to one of Black Power. While many inside and outside the SNCC felt this completely derailed all of their past efforts, this shift "shared common goals and objectives" with the heroic phase of the Civil Rights Movement. Today's libraries face countless changes internally and externally, creating many of the same confused and angry feelings mentioned above. Recognizing this fact is one of the best ways to manage the inevitable, helping library staff and stakeholders to view change as an opportunity for growth.[10]

- Libraries are for all. "A State of its instrumentality may, of course, regulate the use of its libraries," Supreme Court Justice Abe Fortas stated in 1966, "but it must do so in a reasonable and non-discriminatory manner, equally applicable to all and administered with equality to all." He then, in a deceptively simple sentence, said something so profound that it could be applied to racial injustice anywhere: "It may not do so as to some and not as to all." Today, the United States can proudly say that their libraries are "freely available to all citizens." In fact, access to information has been declared a fundamental human right. The Freedom Libraries helped the country get there. Along with providing many with their "first meaningful contact with books and libraries," the Freedom Libraries during the Civil Rights Movement offered basic human acceptance. This is their greatest legacy.[11]

This legacy continues today. In 2016, Chicago native Charles Alexander Preston created the Black History Month Library—a free resource found on Google Drive. "Initially the project was aimed at democratizing information and creating a free resource for those who've been robbed of their history," Preston posted online. "I wanted to honor Carter G. Woodson and the stories I heard of the reading rooms, where enslaved Africans were kept on the course of the underground railroad and some were taught to read. I thought about my five-year-old self being exposed to George Washington— a slave owner—before knowing the wonders of Robert F. Williams, Harriet Tubman, Gabriel Prosser, Denmark Vesey, and various others. I wanted to show my people how beautifully rich and extensive our history is with something anyone can access."[12]

This wasn't easy. Preston spent any free hour he had creating and curating this unique digital library, burning up hard drives and servers along the way. The library ran on donations, and every dollar was used to keep it up and running.

And it was used! Teachers and principals and students all sought information from the works made available by Preston. Some school officials incorporated its use into their curriculum; others credit the library with helping them finish graduate school. It also featured source material not typically available or mentioned during Black History Month, such as Black Communism or the Black Deaf Experience.

Sadly, the Black History Month Library no longer exists. Preston was presented with a cease and desist letter in January of 2019, citing violation of digital copyright laws. He remains happy that he was able to help and inspire so many people, and in return hopes they remember it was free to all.

The long dream continues.

Notes

Preface

1. Murray Kempton, *New York Post*, 1956.

Introduction

1. "Baby Narrowly Escapes Ala. Nightriders Shots," *Jet* 23 (September 23, 1965): 6.

2. Karen Joyce Cook, *Freedom Libraries in the 1964 Mississippi Freedom Summer Project: A History* (Tuscaloosa: University of Alabama Press, 2008), 2, 3.

3. Ibid.

4. Martin Luther King Jr., *The Autobiography of Martin Luther King Jr.*, ed. Clayborne Carson (New York: Warner Books, 2001), 350.

Chapter One

1. Wayne A. Wiegand, *Part of Our Lives: A People's History of the American Public Library* (New York: Oxford University Press, 2016), 145, 146; transcript, Annie L. McPheeters, Oral History Interview with Kathryn L. Nasstrom, June 8, 1992, Georgia Government Documentation Program, Georgia State University Library, pp. 44–46; Clayborne

Carson, email message to author, June 15, 2015. The coincidence of King requesting Gandhi books as a child appears doubtful, and I originally felt McPheeters's recollection of the incident to be suspect. It is not mentioned in the vast literature of King, and King himself does not mention it in any of his autobiographical writings. However, further research has uncovered that the adult education program at the Auburn Branch Library had run several programs about Gandhi and his movement, acquiring supporting material about Gandhi during the same time frame that King requested them. Also, Dr. Clayborne Carson, the founding director of the Martin Luther King Jr. Research and Education Institute at Stanford University, feels in all probability this event did occur. I remain indebted to him for changing my mind.

2. Transcript, Annie L. McPheeters, Oral History Interview with Kathryn L. Nasstrom, June 8, 1992, pp. 44–46.

3. David M. Battles, *The History of Public Library Access for African Americans in the South or Leaving the Plow Behind* (Lanham, MD: Scarecrow Press, 2009), 44.

4. Transcript, Annie L. McPheeters, Oral History Interview with Kathryn L. Nasstrom, June 8, 1992, p. 25.

5. Wiegand, *Part of Our Lives*, 27.

6. Hiller C. Wellman, "What the American Library Association Has Become," *Wilson Library Bulletin*, December 1916, 48.

7. Debbie Z. Harwell, *Wednesdays in Mississippi: Proper Ladies Working for Radical Change* (Oxford: University of Mississippi Press, 2014), 6.

8. Kathleen de la Pena McCook, *Introduction to Public Librarianship* (New York: Neal-Schuman, 2011), 164; Frederick Stielow, "Reconsidering Arsenals of a Democratic Culture," in *Libraries & Democracy: The Cornerstones of Liberty,* ed. Nancy C. Kranich (Chicago: American Library Association, 2001), 12.

9. Shane Hand, "Transmitting Whiteness: Librarians, Children and Race, 1900–1930s" (master's thesis, University of Southern Mississippi, 2011), 4.

10. Patterson Toby Graham, *The Right to Read: Segregation and Civil Rights in Alabama's Public Libraries* (Tuscaloosa: University of Alabama Press, 2002), 72.

11. "Annals of the Civil Rights Movement: 60 Years Ago," *Journal of Blacks in Higher Education* 25 (Autumn 1999): 29.

12. Samuel W. Tucker, "Letter from Samuel W. Tucker to Alexandria Librarian," *Jim Crow Lived Here,* accessed February 9, 2018, http://jim crowlivedhere.org/items/show/23.

13. S. J. Ackerman, "The Trials of S.W. Tucker," *Washington Post,* June 11, 2000, W14.

14. Graham, *The Right to Read,* 1; "Negro Ministers Desegregate Public Library," *Spartanburg Herald Journal,* September 17, 1963.

15. Rice Estes, "Segregated Libraries," *Library Journal,* December 15, 1960, 4421–22.

16. "US Commission on Civil Rights Reports on Southern Libraries," *Library Journal* (October–December 1962): 188–91.

17. Martin Luther King Jr., "Loving Your Enemies," in *The Papers of Martin Luther King, Jr., Volume IV: Symbol of the Movement,* ed. Clayborne Carson (Berkeley: University of California Press, 2000), 331.

CHAPTER TWO

1. Sarai G. Zitter, *Memoirs of a Fortunate Life: The Evolution of an Activist* (Baltimore: PublishAmerica, 2011), 130.

2. Sherry Zitter, email message to author, March 20, 2018.

3. Ibid.

4. Wilson Gee, "The Rural South," *Journal of Social Forces* (November 1924): 713–17.

5. William Couch Jr., "Rural Education in Mississippi," *Journal of Negro Education* (Spring 1952): 226.

6. Kenneth O'Reilly, *Racial Matters: The FBI's Secret File on Black America, 1960–1972* (New York: Free Press, 1991), 11.

7. Mary U. Rothrock, "Library Development in the Southeast," *Bulletin of the American Library Association: Papers and Proceedings of the Forty-Fifth Annual Meeting of the American Library Association* (July 1923): 117.

8. Mary B. Palmer, "County Libraries for the South," *Bulletin of the American Library Association: Papers and Proceedings of the Forty-Fifth Annual Meeting of the American Library Association* (July 1923): 142.

9. George T. Settle, "Work with Negroes Round Table," *Bulletin of the American Library Association: Papers and Proceedings of the Forty-Fifth Annual Meeting of the American Library Association* (July 1923): 275.

10. Ibid.

11. Louis R. Wilson, "Library Service in Rural Areas," *Journal of Social Forces* 15, no. 4 (May 1937): 527.

12. Ibid.

13. University Library Survey, *People without Books: An Analysis of Library Services in Mississippi* (University: Bureau of Public Administration, University of Mississippi, 1950), 16.

14. Ibid., 9.

15. *Sixteenth Biennial Report of the Mississippi Library Commission, July 1, 1955–June 30, 1957* (State of Mississippi, 1957), 3.

16. Ibid.; *Seventeenth Biennial Report of the Mississippi Library Commission, July 1, 1957–June 30, 1959* (State of Mississippi, 1959), 9.

17. *Fifteenth Biennial Report of the Mississippi Library Commission, July 1, 1953–June 30, 1955* (State of Mississippi, 1955), 13.

18. Ibid.

19. "House Approves More Appropriations," *Clarion-Ledger*, March 1, 1956, 10.

20. Karen Cook, "Struggles Within: Lura G. Currier, the Mississippi Library Commission, and Library Services to African Americans," *Information & Culture* 48, no. 1 (2013): 143; Donald G. Davis Jr. and Cheryl Knott Malone, "Reading for Liberation: The Role of Libraries in the 1964 Mississippi Freedom Summer Project," in *Untold Stories: Civil Rights, Libraries, and Black Librarianship*, ed. John Mark Tucker (Champaign: Graduate School of Library and Information Sciences, University of Illinois, 1998), 120.

21. Cook, "Struggles Within," 140.

22. Ibid., 148–49.

23. Martin Luther King Jr., *Why We Can't Wait* (Boston: Beacon Press, 2010), 23.

24. Lura Gibbons Currier, "The Defense Never Rests," *ALA Bulletin* 60, no. 7 (July–August 1966): 705.

25. Dennis Thomison, *A History of the American Library Association, 1876-1972* (Chicago: American Library Association, 1978), 213.

26. David Halberstam, *The Children* (New York: Fawcett Press, 1999), 405; King, *Why We Can't Wait*, 92; Sally Belfrage, *Freedom Summer* (Charlottesville: University of Virginia Press, 1999), 45.

27. "Present Books," *Clarion-Ledger*, February 21, 1960, 21.

28. "Present Books," *Clarion-Ledger*, September 11, 1986, 80; Neil R. McMillen, *The Citizens' Council: Organized Resistance to the Second Reconstruction* (Urbana: University of Illinois Press, 1994), 241–43; "WCC Includes Segregated Heaven in High School Essay Material," *The Delta Democrat-Times*, October 9, 1958, 2.

29. McMillen, *The Citizens' Council*, 360.

30. Ibid., 242.

31. "WCC Includes Segregated Heaven in High School Essay Material," *The Delta Democrat-Times*, October 9, 1958, 2.

32. McMillen, *The Citizens' Council*, 243.

33. "Citizens Councils Teach White Supremacy in State High Schools," *The Delta Democrat-Times*, April 24, 1958, 1; McMillen, *The Citizens' Council*, 243.

34. "Miss Mac, 85, Is Still a Patriot with a Passion," *Clarion-Ledger*, September 2, 1982, 66.

35. David Halberstam, *The Children* (New York: Fawcett Press, 1999), 389; Cook, "Struggles Within," 141.

36. Taylor Branch, *Parting the Waters: America in the King Years, 1954–1963* (New York: Simon & Schuster, 1988), 495.

37. Ibid., 498.

38. Ibid., 330.

39. Karla F. C. Holloway, *Bookmarks: Reading in Black and White: A Memoir* (New Brunswick: Rutgers University Press, 2006), 7.

40. David Dennis, "An Abortion for a Pregnant State," *Congress of Racial Equality Papers, 1941–1967,* State Historical Society of Wisconsin, Madison, 1963, p. 4.

41. Ibid.

42. Rita Schwerner, "Letter to Anne Braden," *Carl and Anne Braden papers, 1928–2006,* State Historical Society of Wisconsin, Madison, January 1964, p. 1.

43. Mickey Schwerner, "Meridian Community Center," *Reports (Weekly) by M. Schwerner and Staff, January–July 1964,* State Historical Society of Wisconsin, Madison, January 1964, p. 19.

44. "Library Project," *Now! The Voice of Freedom,* May 4, 1964, 3.

45. U.S. Department of Justice, Federal Bureau of Investigation, "Communist Infiltration of Student Non-Violent Coordinating Committee," 1964; *Council of Federated Organizations*, "Six Civil Rights Workers Accused of Stealing Books; Freedom School Books Said to 'Advocate Overthrow of Govt.': Two Kangaroo Courts in Two Days," State Historical Society of Wisconsin, Madison, May 1964, p. 1.

46. Emmie Schrader Adams, "From Africa to Mississippi," in *Deep in Our Hearts: Nine White Women in the Freedom Movement* (Athens: University of Georgia Press, 2002), 314.

47. John Fischer, "The Editor's Easy Chair: A Small Band of Practical Heroes," *Harper's,* October 1963, 5.

48. *Council of Federated Organizations*, "Progress and Problems of the COFO Community Centers," State Historical Society of Wisconsin, Madison, Summer, 1964, p. 68.

49. "First CORE Community Center in Mississippi," *CORE-lator,* February 1964, 4.

50. Karen Cook, *Freedom Libraries in the 1964 Mississippi Freedom Summer Project: A History* (Tuscaloosa: University of Alabama Press, 2008), 92.

51. Bruce Watson, *Freedom Summer: The Savage Summer That Made Mississippi Burn and Made America a Democracy* (New York: Penguin Books, 2010), 8.

52. Shirley Bates, interview with author, March 17, 2018.

Chapter Three

1. Gwendolyn Zohara Simmons, "From Little Memphis Girl to Mississippi Amazon," in *Hands on the Freedom Plow: Personal Accounts by Women in SNCC*, ed. Faith S. Holsaert (Chicago: University of Illinois Press, 2012), 24.

2. Ibid., 26.

3. Harry G. Lefever, *Undaunted by the Fight: Spelman College and the Civil Rights Movement, 1957–1967* (Macon: Mercer University Press, 2005), 197; Gwendolyn Zohara Simmons, interview with author, February 10, 2018. Simmons did reconcile with her mother after Freedom Summer, but not so much with her grandmother. In our interview she stated,

> My grandmother would never concede that I had done the right thing by dropping out of school and joining SNCC. Even when I went back to college 20 years later and invited her to my graduation, she said she was too old to travel to Philadelphia, but she also said: "It is about Time!" She also lived to learn that I had gotten my M.A. but she still seemed to feel that I had let her down. After a while I stopped trying to get her to agree that I had done the right thing.
>
> I got over it as I realized more and more what going to college meant to her. It was something she so desperately wanted for herself. As she had only been able to complete the 6th grade, though she wanted to go beyond, there was no school for African Americans beyond the 6th grade in her part of the county in Earl, Arkansas. She was living her dream through me.

4. Simmons, interview with author, February 10, 2018.

5. Bruce Watson, *Freedom Summer: The Savage Season of 1964 That Made Mississippi Burn and Made America a Democracy* (New York: Penguin Books, 2011), 56.

6. *Council of Federated Organizations*, "Security Handbook," State Historical Society of Wisconsin, Madison, July 1964, p. 3.

7. William Bradford Huie, *Three Lives for Mississippi* (New York: Whitney Communications Corporation, 1965), 10.

8. Penny Patch, "SNCC WATS Reports," State Historical Society of Wisconsin, Madison, July 7, 1964, p. 10.

9. Casey Hayden, "SNCC WATS Reports," State Historical Society of Wisconsin, Madison, July 5, 1964, p. 7.

10. Penny Patch, "SNCC WATS Reports," State Historical Society of Wisconsin, Madison, July 6, 1964, p. 10.

11. Simmons, interview with author, February 10, 2018.

12. Ibid.

13. Ibid.

14. John W. Herz, "This Is the Story of My Two Weeks as a Civil Rights Lawyer in Mississippi in July 1964" (San Francisco: Westwind Writers, 1964), 10.

15. Faith S. Holsaert, "*Hands on the Freedom Plow* Author Event," Presentation at Modern Times Bookstore, San Francisco, CA, December 12, 2010.

16. Simmons, interview with author, February 10, 2018.

17. Gwendolyn Zohara Simmons, "From Little Memphis Girl to Mississippi Amazon," in *Hands on the Freedom Plow: Personal Accounts by Women in SNCC,* ed. Faith S. Holsaert (Chicago: University of Illinois Press, 2012), 28.

18. Simmons, interview with author, February 10, 2018.

19. Ibid.; Anthony J. Onwuegbuzi et al., *Library Anxiety: Theory, Research, and Applications* (New York: Scarecrow Press, 2004), 25. The authors define *library anxiety* as "an uncomfortable feeling or emotional disposition, experienced in a library setting, which has cognitive, affective, physiological, and behavioural ramifications." Symptoms include "apprehension, frustration, and learned helplessness . . . tension, fear, uneasiness, negative self-defeating thoughts, feelings of uncertainty and mental disorganization." These reported results are from college and university students—whom one can assume are mostly middle class and have grown up being welcomed in libraries if not using them directly.

20. Simmons, interview with author, February 10, 2018.

21. Sanford Leigh, "Special to Students and Young People of Ruleville, Indianola, and Drew," State Historical Society of Wisconsin, Madison, 1964, p. 3.

22. Simmons, "From Little Memphis Girl to Mississippi Amazon," 32.

23. Bob Beyers, "SNCC WATS Reports," State Historical Society of Wisconsin, Madison, July 16, 1964, p. 7; Margaret Rose, "SNCC WATS

Reports," State Historical Society of Wisconsin, Madison, July 19, 1964, p. 8.

24. Virginia Steele, "A New Librarian on the Mississippi Summer Project, 1964," *California Librarian* (1965): 145–78.

25. Ibid., 145.

26. Donald G. Davis Jr., and Cheryl Knott Malone, "Reading for Liberation: The Role of Libraries in the 1964 Mississippi Freedom Summer Project," in *Untold Stories: Civil Rights, Libraries, and Black Librarianship*, ed. John Mark Tucker (Champaign: Graduate School of Library and Information Sciences, University of Illinois, 1998), 113.

27. Steele, "A New Librarian on the Mississippi Summer Project, 1964," 146.

28. Davis and Malone, "Reading for Liberation," 113.

29. Virginia Steele, "Greenville, July 21," in *Letters from Mississippi: Reports from Civil Rights Volunteers and Freedom School Poetry of the 1964 Freedom Summer*, ed. Elizabeth Martinez (Brookline, MA: Zephyr Press, 2002), 128.

30. Steele, "A New Librarian on the Mississippi Summer Project, 1964," 148.

31. Ibid.

32. Yasuhiro Katagiri, *The Mississippi State Sovereignty Commission: Civil Rights and States' Rights* (Jackson: University Press of Mississippi, 2001), 6. Since the Freedom School and Library was located at 920 Nelson Street, the commission may not have hired the best agents.

33. *Mississippi State Sovereignty Commission*, "Jackson and Greenville, Mississippi, August 15, 1964," Sovereignty Commission Online, www.mdah.ms.gov/arrec/digital_archives/sovcom.

34. Karen Cook, *Freedom Libraries in the 1964 Mississippi Freedom Summer Project: A History* (Tuscaloosa: University of Alabama Press, 2008), 205.

35. Ibid., 221.

36. Ibid., 191; Davis and Malone, "Reading for Liberation," 120.

37. Cook, *Freedom Libraries in the 1964 Mississippi Freedom Summer Project*, 206.

38. Steele, "A New Librarian on the Mississippi Summer Project, 1964," 149.

39. Ibid.

40. Ibid.

41. Virginia Steele, "Memorandum to Library Workers, August 7, 1964," State Historical Society of Wisconsin, Madison, July 28, 1964, pp. 1, 3.

42. Steele, "A New Librarian on the Mississippi Summer Project, 1964," 150.

43. Sally Belfrage, *Freedom Summer* (Charlottesville: University of Virginia Press, 1999), 38.

44. Ibid., 39.

45. Lorna D. Smith, "Thoughts on My Mississippi Project," in "Diary and Notes, 1964, Jun-Aug.," ed. Sally Belfrage, State Historical Society of Wisconsin, Madison, 1964, p. 1.

46. Ibid., 3.

47. Ibid.

48. Ibid., 47–48; Peniel E. Joseph, *Stokely: A Life* (New York: Basic Civitas, 2014), 112.

49. Smith, "Thoughts on My Mississippi Project," 4.

50. Ibid.

51. Ibid.

52. Ibid.

53. Belfrage, *Freedom Summer*, 25.

54. Ibid., 29; Sally Belfrage, *Un-American Activities: A Memoir of the Fifties* (New York: HarperCollins, 1994), 245.

55. Belfrage, *Freedom Summer*, 35, 42.

56. Ibid., 47.

57. Ibid., 115.

58. Ibid., 67.

59. Sally Belfrage, "Diary and Notes, 1964, Jun–Aug.," State Historical Society of Wisconsin, Madison, 1964, pp. 54, 92.

60. Belfrage, *Freedom Summer*, 211–14.

61. Belfrage, "Diary and Notes, 1964, Jun–Aug.," 86.

62. Belfrage, *Freedom Summer*, 204.

63. Belfrage, "Diary and Notes, 1964, Jun–Aug.," 103. Belfrage would have no doubt laughed at being called "that great American." With her parents being labeled communist spies and deported, she stated in her memoir, "I'm an un-American. . . . I haven't even got a country, really, since having one turns out to be not a given at after all, but conditional on good behavior ('Go back to Russia!')." Her father actually did turn out to be a spy, but for the British government.

64. Belfrage, *Freedom Summer*, 232.

65. John O'Neal, "A General Prospectus for the Establishment of a Free Southern Theater," in *The Free Southern Theater, by the Free Southern Theater: A Documentary of the South's Radical Black Theater, with Journals, Letters, Poetry, Essays, and a Play Written by Those Who Built It*, ed.

Thomas C. Dent, Richard Schechner, and Gilbert Moses (Indianapolis: Bobbs-Merrill, 1969), 22.

66. Shirley Martin Bates, interview with author, March 17, 2018.

67. Ibid.

68. Ibid.

69. "Civil Rights Driving Tour," *McComb Legacies*, February 2009, 6.

70. Denise Nicholas, *Freshwater Road* (Evanston, IL: Agate, 2005), 382.

71. Denise Nicholas, email message to author, March 21, 2018.

CHAPTER FOUR

1. Mendy Samstein, "The Murder of a Community," *The Student Voice,* September 23, 1964, 2.

2. Council of Federated Organizations, *Mississippi Black Paper* (Jackson: University of Mississippi Press, 2017), 92.

3. Dennis Sweeney, "Copy of Affidavit," SNCC, McComb, 1964.

4. David Halberstam, *The Children* (New York: Fawcett Press, 1999), 404.

5. Shirley Martin Bates, interview with author, March 17, 2018.

6. Ibid.

7. Jon N. Hale and William Sturkey, eds., *To Write in the Light of Freedom: The Newspapers of the 1964 Mississippi Freedom Schools* (Jackson: University of Mississippi Press, 2015).

8. Ibid., 117.

9. William Bradford Huie, *Three Lives for Mississippi* (New York: Whitney Communications Corporation, 1965), 37.

10. Ibid., 45.

11. Mickey Schwerner, "Meridian Community Center," *Reports (Weekly) by M. Schwerner and Staff, January–July 1964,* State Historical Society of Wisconsin, Madison, January 1964, p. 34.

12. Huie, *Three Lives for Mississippi*, 49.

13. Schwerner, "Meridian Community Center," 14.

14. Ibid.

15. Ibid.

16. Ibid., 28.

17. Ibid., 34.

18. Huie, *Three Lives for Mississippi*, 53; Schwerner, "Meridian Community Center," 42.

19. Ibid., 7, 21, 36.

20. Ibid., 25.

21. Huie, *Three Lives for Mississippi*, 63.

22. Schwerner, "Meridian Community Center," 21, 29, 36.

23. Doug McAdam, *Freedom Summer* (New York: Oxford University Press, 1988), 257.

24. Taylor Branch, *Pillar of Fire: America in the King Years, 1963–65* (New York: Simon & Schuster, 1998), 362; Kenneth O'Reilly, *Racial Matters: The FBI's Secret File on Black America, 1960–1972* (New York: Free Press, 1991), 164.

25. Huie, *Three Lives for Mississippi*, 50.

26. Patti Miller, "Letter from Mississippi to Family and Friends," *Keeping History Alive*, accessed June 15, 2018, www.keepinghistoryalive.com/letters.html.

27. Patti Miller, "Living with Dying," unpublished manuscript (Fairfield, undated); Patti Miller, interview with author, February 10, 2018.

28. Miller, "Living with Dying."

29. Patti Miller, interview with author, February 10, 2018.

30. Patti Miller, "Dirt," unpublished manuscript (Fairfield, undated).

31. Ibid.

32. Patti Miller, "August 7, 1964," *Keeping History Alive*, accessed June 15, 2018, www.keepinghistoryalive.com/journal-aug7.html; Patti Miller, interview with author, February 10, 2018, 47; "Changing History," *Des Moines Register*, June 22, 2014, OP-1.

33. "Amazed at Forgiveness of Negro Community," *Des Moines Tribune*, September 23, 1964, 37; "Views Racial Situation after Mississippi Project," *Drake-Times Delphic*, September 25, 1964.

34. Robert Brookins Gore, "Dear Dr. Tarachow," in "Correspondence General, 1964," State Historical Society of Wisconsin, Madison, 1964, p. 58; Robert Brookins Gore, "Dear Cohorts in Freedom," in "Correspondence General, 1964," State Historical Society of Wisconsin, Madison, 1964, p. 50.

35. Marvin Rich, "To CORE Chapter Leaders," in "SEDFRE-Community Center Proposals, Organization and Plans for Center, 1964–65," State Historical Society of Wisconsin, Madison, 1964, p. 1.

36. Rita Schwerner, "Community Center," in "SEDFRE-Community Center Proposals, Organization and Plans for Center, 1964–65," State Historical Society of Wisconsin, Madison, 1964, p. 18.

37. Abe Osheroff and Jim Boebel, "Dream in a Bean Field," *Nation*, September 5, 1964, 514.

38. Ibid.

39. Allard K. Lowenstein, *The Brutal Mandate: A Journey to Southwest Africa* (New York: Macmillan, 1962), 261. In an awful twist, Lowenstein was shot to death on March 14, 1980, by Dennis Sweeney, who suffered a concussion in the McComb Freedom House bombing. Sue Sojourner [Lorenzi] and Cheryl Reitan, *Thunder of Freedom: Black Leadership and the Transformation of 1960s Mississippi* (Lexington: University of Kentucky Press, 2013), 9.

40. Ibid., 56.

41. "SNCC WATS Reports," State Historical Society of Wisconsin, Madison, November 1, 1964, p. 92.

42. "Mileston Opens Community Center," *The Student Voice*, October 28, 1964, 3.

43. Sojourner and Reitan, *Thunder of Freedom*, 70.

44. Anna Delany, "Everyday Heroes: The Civil Rights Movement in Holmes County, Mississippi" (master's thesis, State University of New York, 2012), 69.

45. Sojourner and Reitan, *Thunder of Freedom*, 208–9; Matt Herron, "Mississippi Headstart," *Take Stock: Images of Change*, accessed June 17, 2018, www.takestockphotos.com/imagepages/imagedetail .php?PSortOrder=10&FolioID=20#.

46. Sojourner and Reitan, *Thunder of Freedom*, 150; Sue Sojourner [Lorenzi], interview with author, February 20, 2018.

47. Osheroff and Boebel, "Dream in a Bean Field," 514; "Mileston Opens Community Center," *The Student Voice*, October 28, 1964, 3; John Dittmer, *Local People: The Struggle for Civil Rights in Mississippi* (Champaign: University of Illinois Press, 1994), 253; Akinyele Omowale Umoja, *We Will Shoot Back: Armed Resistance in the Mississippi Freedom Movement* (New York: New York University Press, 2013), 75.

48. Sojourner and Reitan, *Thunder of Freedom*, 70.

49. Jonathan L. Walton, "Dignity as a Weapon of Love," in *To Shape a New World: Essays on the Political Philosophy of Martin Luther King Jr.*, ed. Tommie Shelby and Brandon M. Terry (Cambridge: Belknap Press, 2018), 347.

50. Sue Sojourner [Lorenzi], interview with author, February 20, 2018; Sojourner and Reitan, *Thunder of Freedom*, 55–56.

51. Sue Sojourner [Lorenzi], interview with author, February 20, 2018.

52. Dittmer, *Local People*, 125; Shirley Ford, "8 Years in Ruleville Central High," in "Ruleville, 1962-1964 n.d.," State Historical Society of Wisconsin, Madison, 1964, p. 84.

53. Eric Moskowitz, "Summer of 1964," *Boston Globe,* August 31, 2014.

54. "SNCC Workers Call Police Bluff," in "Ruleville, 1962–1964 n.d.," State Historical Society of Wisconsin, Madison, 1964, p. 34.

55. Ellen Wolfe, email message to author, March 21, 2018.

56. "Their Dream Is Not to Be Nervous," *Mademoiselle,* November 1964, 202; Kirsty Powell, "A Report, Mainly on Ruleville Freedom School, Summer Project, 1964," *Education and Democracy,* accessed June 17, 2018, www.educationanddemocracy.org/FSCfiles/B_15_ReportRuleville.htm.

57. Moskowitz, "Summer of 1964."

58. Ibid.

59. Leonard Edwards, "Harassment by Private Parties," "Ruleville, 1962–1964 n.d," State Historical Society of Wisconsin, Madison, 1964, p. 53; Danielle Ziri, "The Untold Story of a Jewish Freedom Rider," *Jerusalem Post,* January 31, 2016, accessed June 17, 2018, www.jpost.com/Diaspora/The-untold-story-of-a-Jewish-Freedom-Rider-443318.

60. "Ruleville Project Meets ATAC," in "Ruleville, 1962–1964 n.d.," State Historical Society of Wisconsin, Madison, 1964, p. 52.

61. "Library Bars SNCC Workers," in "Carl and Ann Braden Papers, 1928–2006," State Historical Society of Wisconsin, Madison, 1964, p. 19.

62. Ibid.

63. "Drew Police Arrest 25 More," in "Ruleville, 1962–1964 n.d.," State Historical Society of Wisconsin, Madison, 1964, p. 48.

64. Ellen Wolfe, email message to author, March 21, 2018; "Drew Police Arrest 25 More," in "Ruleville, 1962–1964 n.d.," State Historical Society of Wisconsin, Madison, 1964, p. 48.

65. Moskowitz, "Summer of 1964."

66. Sheldon Stromquist, "Vicksburg Freedom House," in *Iowans Return to Freedom Summer, 2015,* dir. Angelo Wulf, DVD; Sheldon Stromquist, "John Dittmer Interview of Sheldon Stromquist," in "Sheldon Stromquist Papers, 1963–1978," State Historical Society of Wisconsin, Madison, 1964, p. 12.

67. Stromquist, "John Dittmer Interview of Sheldon Stromquist," 12.

68. Karen Cook, *Freedom Libraries in the 1964 Mississippi Freedom Summer Project: A History* (Tuscaloosa: University of Alabama Press, 2008), 251; "News From The Vicksburg Project," in "Gould—Richard N. Gould Papers, 1963–1965," State Historical Society of Wisconsin, Madison, 1964, p. 4; Donald G. Davis Jr. and Cheryl Knott Malone, "Reading for Liberation: The Role of Libraries in the 1964 Mississippi

Freedom Summer Project," in *Untold Stories: Civil Rights, Libraries, and Black Librarianship*, ed. John Mark Tucker (Champaign: Graduate School of Library and Information Sciences, University of Illinois, 1998), 120.

69. "Dear People," in "Dunlap—Correspondence by Bryan Dunlap, 1964–1965," State Historical Society of Wisconsin, Madison, 1964, pp. 6, 43.

70. Ibid.

71. "Vicksburg COFO Library Needs and Budget for the Coming Year," in "Gould—Richard N. Gould Papers, 1963–1965," State Historical Society of Wisconsin, Madison, 1964, p. 1.

72. Ibid.

73. Bruce Watson, *Freedom Summer: The Savage Season of 1964 That Made Mississippi Burn and Made America a Democracy* (New York: Penguin Books, 2011), 185.

74. Stromquist, "John Dittmer Interview of Sheldon Stromquist," 7; Watson, *Freedom Summer*, 186; "Bryan Dunlap Writes to Leonia," in "Dunlap—Correspondence by Bryan Dunlap, 1964–1965," State Historical Society of Wisconsin, Madison, 1964, 2; Dittmer, *Local People*, 262.

75. Drew Pearson, "Vicksburg Is Now Mississippi's Most Moderate City Racially," *Clarion-Ledger*, October 15, 1964, 12.

76. Stromquist, "John Dittmer Interview of Sheldon Stromquist," 19; Watson, *Freedom Summer*, 232–35; "WATS Reports," in "Lucile Montgomery Papers, 1963–1967," State Historical Society of Wisconsin, Madison, 1964, pp. 189–99.

77. "Bombing at the Vicksburg Freedom House," in "Dunlap—Correspondence by Bryan Dunlap, 1964–1965," State Historical Society of Wisconsin, Madison, 1964, p. 58.

78. Ibid.

79. "Dear Mom, Dad, and Jeff," in "SAVF Council of Federated Organizations (COFO) papers," State Historical Society of Wisconsin, Madison, 1964, p. 68.

80. Stromquist, "Vicksburg Freedom House."

81. Ibid.

82. Mendy Samstein, "The Murder of a Community," *The Student Voice*, September 23, 1964, 2.

83. "Bombing at the Vicksburg Freedom House," 58; "Dear People," 55.

84. "Dear Pa," in "Dunlap—Correspondence by Bryan Dunlap, 1964–1965," State Historical Society of Wisconsin, Madison, 1964, p. 69.

85. Frederick W. Heinze, "The Freedom Libraries: A Wedge in a Closed Society," *Library Journal,* April 15, 1965, p. 39.

86. "Dear Fritz," in "Dunlap—Correspondence by Bryan Dunlap, 1964–1965," State Historical Society of Wisconsin, Madison, 1964, pp. 63, 71.

87. Ibid., 63.

88. Jon N. Hale, "The Struggle Begins Early: Head Start and the Mississippi Freedom Movement," *History of Education Quarterly* 52, no. 4 (2012): 506; Miriam Braverman, "Mississippi Summer," *School Library Journal* (November 1965): 31.

89. Halberstam, *The Children,* 288.

Chapter Five

1. Doug McAdam, email message to author, July 2, 2018.

2. David Halberstam, *The Children* (New York: Fawcett Press, 1999), 288, 411, 417–18.

3. Charles W. Eagles, *Outside Agitator: Jon Daniels and the Civil Rights Movement in Alabama* (Tuscaloosa: University of Alabama Press, 2000), 89, 126; Hasan Kwame Jeffries, *Bloody Lowndes: Civil Rights and Black Power in Alabama's Black Belt* (New York: New York University Press, 2009), 8, 213.

4. Jeffries, *Bloody Lowndes,* 60.

5. Kenneth R. Johnson, "The Early Library Movement in Alabama," *Journal of Library History* 6, no. 2 (1971): 120–31.

6. Annabel K. Stephens, "The Founding and Early Development of Alabama Public Libraries: A Content Analysis of 116 of the Libraries' Written Histories," *Alabama Librarian* 54, no. 2 (2004): 32–38.

7. Ibid.

8. Eliza Atkins Gleason, "Facing the Dilemma of Public Library Service for Negroes," *Library Quarterly* 15, no. 4 (1945): 339–44.

9. Kayla Barrett, and Barbara A. Bishop, "Integration and the Alabama Library Association: Not So Black and White," *Libraries & Culture* 33, no. 2 (1998): 142–61.

10. Halberstam, *The Children,* 416, 426–28; Taylor Branch, *Pillar of Fire: America in the King Years, 1963–65* (New York: Simon & Schuster, 1998), 107; Frye Gaillard, *Cradle of Freedom: Alabama and the Movement That Changed America* (Tuscaloosa: University of Alabama Press, 2004), 176.

11. Maria Varela, "Time to Get Ready," in *Hands on the Freedom Plow: Personal Accounts by Women in SNCC,* ed. Faith S. Holsaert (Chicago: University of Illinois Press, 2012), 558; Paul Murray, "54 Miles to Freedom: Catholics Were Prominent in 1965 Selma March," *National Catholic Reporter,* March 17, 2015, 9.

12. Murray, "54 Miles to Freedom," 9.

13. Ibid.

14. Maria Varela, email message to author, June 27, 2018.

15. Martin Luther King Jr., "Voices," in *The Unfinished Agenda of the Selma-Montgomery Voting Rights March,* ed. Dara N. Byrne and the editors of *Black Issues in Higher Education* (Hoboken: John Wiley & Sons, 2005), 11–12.

16. Ibid., 13.

17. The Student Nonviolent Coordinating Committee, *The Selma Literacy Project: A Report for the Year 1963–1964,* State Historical Society of Wisconsin, Madison, 1967, p. 3: Bruce Hartford, *The Selma Voting Rights Struggle and the March to Montgomery* (San Francisco: West Wind Writers, 2014), 199.

18. Maria Varela, *Prospectus: Selma Literacy Project,* author's personal papers, 1963.

19. Ibid.

20. The Student Nonviolent Coordinating Committee, *The Selma Literacy Project,* 3.

21. Ibid., 4.

22. Ibid., 4.

23. Varela, "Time to Get Ready," 560.

24. "Johnson Signs Civil Rights Act 1964," *History.com,* last modified July 2, 2009, www.history.com/this-day-in-history/johnson-signs-civil-rights-act; Jerry Demuth, "Total Segregation: Black Belt Alabama," *The Commonweal,* August 7, 1964.

25. Varela, "Time to Get Ready," 571: Maria Varela, email message to author, June 27, 2018. While the literacy project didn't work in Alabama, it had great success in Mississippi. Varela shifted the focus to adult education and produced a series of books and filmstrips titled *Something of Our Own.* These works were so popular that copies eventually made their way to Alabama. Today she is a professor, an author, a community organizer, and an award-winning photographer.

26. Jacintha U. Eze, "Role of the Public Library in Adult Continuing Education and Life Long Learning in Nigeria," *The Nigerian Academic Forum* (November 2011): 73–74; Lisa Krolak, "The Role of Libraries

in the Creation of Literate Environments," paper commissioned for the *EFA Global Monitoring Report 2006, Literacy for Life* (2005): 3; Derrick Darby, "A Vindication of Voting Rights," in *To Shape a New World: Essays on the Political Philosophy of Martin Luther King, Jr.*, ed. Tommie Shelby and Brandon M. Terry (Cambridge: Belknap Press of Harvard University Press, 2018), 166.

27. Branch, *Pillar of Fire*, 580.

28. Halberstam, *The Children*, 513–14.

29. David Garrow, *Bearing the Cross: Martin Luther King Jr., and the Southern Christian Leadership Conference* (New York: Perennial Classics, 2004), 403.

30. Peter Kellman, "Freedom Movement Memories," unpublished paper.

31. Ibid.

32. Ibid.

33. Peter Kellman, interview with author, June 19, 2013.

34. Ibid.

35. Bruce Hartford, email message to author, March 29, 2013.

36. Charles Fager, email message to author, June 19, 2013.

37. Kellman, interview with author, June 19, 2013.

38. Karen Cook, *Freedom Libraries in the 1964 Mississippi Freedom Summer Project: A History* (Tuscaloosa: University of Alabama Press, 2008), xviii; Myrna Wood, email message to author, June 19, 2013.

39. Kellman, interview with author, June 19, 2013.

40. Ibid.

41. Ibid.; Dennis Coleman, email message to author, June 7, 2013; Fager, email message to author, June 19, 2013.

42. Hartford, email message to author, March 29, 2013; Kellman, interview with author, June 19, 2013.

43. Patterson Toby Graham, *The Right to Read: Segregation and Civil Rights in Alabama's Public Libraries* (Tuscaloosa: University of Alabama Press, 2002), 115.

44. Coleman, email message to author, June 7, 2013.

45. Kellman, interview with author, June 19, 2013.

46. Ibid.

47. Willy S. Leventhal, *The Scope of Freedom: The Leadership of Hosea Williams with Dr. King's Summer '65 Student Volunteers* (Montgomery: Challenge Publishing, 2005), 439–41.

48. Hartford, email message to author, March 29, 2013.

49. Kellman, interview with author, June 19, 2013.

50. Ibid.

51. Jack Mendelsohn, *The Martyrs: Sixteen Who Gave Their Lives for Racial Justice* (New York: Harper and Row, 1966), 208.

52. Paul T. Murray, "Richard Morrisroe's Civil Rights Journey," *Journal of Illinois History* 18 (Summer 2015): 83–84.

53. Ibid., 86; Eagles, *Outside Agitator*, 29.

54. Murray, "Richard Morrisroe's Civil Rights Journey," 87.

55. Ibid.

56. Ibid., 88–89.

57. Taylor Branch, *At Canaan's Edge: America in the King Years, 1965–68* (New York: Simon & Schuster, 2007), 281.

58. Ibid., 290: Eagles, *Outside Agitator*, 169.

59. Murray, "Richard Morrisroe's Civil Rights Journey," 90.

60. Branch, *At Canaan's Edge*, 281.

61. Eagles, *Outside Agitator*, 175.

62. Branch, *At Canaan's Edge*, 303.

63. Gloria House, "We'll Never Turn Back," in *Hands on the Freedom Plow: Personal Accounts by Women in SNCC*, ed. Faith S. Holsaert (Chicago: University of Illinois Press, 2012), 507.

64. Murray, "Richard Morrisroe's Civil Rights Journey," 94: Branch, *At Canaan's Edge*, 304; Frye Gaillard, *Cradle of Freedom: Alabama and the Movement that Changed America* (Tuscaloosa: University of Alabama Press, 2004), 282.

65. Branch, *At Canaan's Edge*, 304. The shooting certainly didn't stop Morrisroe from leading an interesting and what appears to be a full life. While his parents were disappointed in him, and his Church more livid than ever (they refused to reinstate him at Saint Columbus), he would end up leaving the priesthood, starting a family (naming his first child after Jonathan Daniels), going to law school, teaching, and earning a PhD. He is currently—at 80—a city planner. He continues to be involved with the Catholic Sisters of Lowndes County outreach, which has an adult literacy program. In 1998 his daughter volunteered there with him.

66. Jeffries, *Bloody Lowndes*, 60.

67. Ibid., 99.

68. Ibid., 100.

69. Willie James McDonald, interview with author, June 26, 2013.

70. Ibid.

71. Ibid.; Jeffries, *Bloody Lowndes*, 82.

72. McDonald, interview with author, June 26, 2013.

73. Ibid. Recollections are hazy here, so they may be conjecture on the author's part. The McDonald family—who have hung on to Morris-

roe's donated Bible for half a century—recall both Daniels and Morrisroe frequenting their home, which held the Hayneville Freedom Library. Morrisroe has no memory of visiting it, and the record of his movements also confirm this. It is more probable that Daniels had visited them, and although he wasn't Catholic, members of the McDonald family attributed the donated Bible as coming from him. In a 2013 meeting with the McDonald family, I was lucky enough to hold Morrisroe's personal Bible, and unlucky enough to have my expensive camera break down.

74. Jeffries, *Bloody Lowndes*, 100.

75. Prathia Hall, "Bloody Selma," in *Hands on the Freedom Plow: Personal Accounts by Women in SNCC*, ed. Faith S. Holsaert (Chicago: University of Illinois Press, 2012), 470–71.

76. Darby, "A Vindication of Voting Rights," 165; Peniel E. Joseph, *Stokely: A Life* (New York: Basic Civitas, 2014).

CHAPTER SIX

1. Timothy J. Lombardo, *Blue-Collar Conservatism: Frank Rizzo's Philadelphia and Populist Politics* (Philadelphia: University of Pennsylvania Press, 2018), 49, 50; Jeff Gammage, "Riot That Forever Changed Philly Neighbourhood," *Washington Times* (Washington, DC), August 30, 2014; Alex Elkins, "Columbia Avenue Riot," *The Encyclopedia of Greater Philadelphia*, accessed October 18, 2018, https://philadelphiaencyclopedia.org/archive/columbia-avenue-riot.

2. Gerald L. Early, *This Is Where I Came In: Black America in the 60s* (Lincoln: University of Nebraska, 2003), 76; Hillary S. Kativa, "What: The Columbia Avenue Riots," *Civil Rights in a Northern City: Philadelphia*, accessed October 18, 2018, http://northerncity.library.temple.edu/exhibits/show/civil-rights-in-a-northern-cit/collections/columbia-avenue-riots/the-columbia-avenue-riots--196; Gammage, "Riot That Forever Changed Philly Neighbourhood," 3; John Elliot Churchville, *Oral History Interview*, by Joseph Monsier, Library of Congress, July 15, 2011; John Elliot Churchville, *Driven: Remembrance, Reflection & Revelation* (Conshohocken, PA: Infinity Press, 2013), 7.

3. Matthew J. Countryman, *Up South: Civil Rights and Black Power in Philadelphia* (Philadelphia: University of Pennsylvania Press, 2003), 184.

4. Countryman, *Up South*, 180–87; Churchville, *Oral History Interview*.

5. Churchville, *Oral History Interview*.

6. Russel John Rickford, *We Are an African People: Independent Education, Black Power, and the Radical Imagination* (New York: Oxford University Press, 2013), 93.

7. John Elliot Churchville, "NSM Freedom Library: A General Statement: Community Action" (New York: Schomburg Center for Research in Black Culture, 1964), 5.

8. Ibid., 3.

9. Churchville, *Oral History Interview*; Countryman, *Up South*, 186.

10. Churchville, *Oral History Interview*.

11. William Strickland, "Northern Student Movement Freedom Library Report" (New York: Schomburg Center for Research in Black Culture, 1964), 1.

12. William Strickland, "Dear Gloria" (New York: Schomburg Center for Research in Black Culture, August 12, 1964), 1. Gloria Davis was James Baldwin's assistant, whom Strickland knew personally.

13. "Dear John Churchville" (New York: Schomburg Center for Research in Black Culture, October 7, 1964), 1.

14. Ibid.

15. James Smart, "A Library Grows in the Rubble," *Sunday Bulletin* (Philadelphia), September 6, 1964.

16. Ibid.

17. Churchville, *Oral History Interview*.

18. John Elliot Churchville, "Description of Present Programs and Projected Improvements" (New York: Schomburg Center for Research in Black Culture, 1964), 1, 2.

19. Ibid.

20. John Elliot Churchville, "Description of Present Programs and Projected Improvements: Neighborhood Tutorial Program" (New York: Schomburg Center for Research in Black Culture, 1964), 2.

21. Ibid.

22. Countryman, *Up South*, 187.

23. John Elliot Churchville, "Description of Present Programs and Projected Improvements: Preschool Program" (New York: Schomburg Center for Research in Black Culture, 1964), 3.

24. "Art and Music Program" (New York: Schomburg Center for Research in Black Culture, n.d.), 1, 2.

25. Ibid.

26. Countryman, *Up South*, 200; Churchville, "NSM Freedom Library: A General Statement: Community Action," 5.

27. Churchville, "Description of Present Programs and Projected Improvements: Neighborhood Youth Program," 5.

28. Ibid.

29. Strickland, "Northern Student Movement Freedom Library Report," 4.

30. Ibid., 3.

31. Churchville, *Oral History Interview*.

32. John Elliot Churchville, "Report from John Churchville: Thursday, June 24th" (New York: Schomburg Center for Research in Black Culture, n.d.), 1.

33. Churchville, *Oral History Interview*.

34. Ibid.

35. Ibid.

36. Countryman, *Up South*, 206.

37. John Elliot Churchville and William Strickland, "Black Unity Movement" (New York: Schomburg Center for Research in Black Culture, February 17, 1965), 1, 2.

38. Churchville, *Oral History Interview*.

39. Ibid.

40. Charyn Sutton, "Minutes of Staff Meeting" (New York: Schomburg Center for Research in Black Culture, October 8, 1965), 2.

41. John Elliot Churchville, email message to author, October 10, 2018.

42. Al Hasbrouck, "Director Explains Freedom Library's Employment Policy," *Temple University News* (Philadelphia), December 17, 1964.

43. Gary R. Adams, "Hate or Caution" (New York: Schomburg Center for Research in Black Culture, n.d.), 2.

44. Ibid.

45. Churchville, email message to author, October 10, 2018.

46. Maria Varela, "Time to Get Ready," in *Hands on the Freedom Plow: Personal Accounts by Women in SNCC*, ed. Faith S. Holsaert (Chicago: University of Illinois Press, 2012), 567; Hasan Kwame Jeffries, "SNCC, Black Power, and Independent Political Party Organizing in Alabama, 1964-1966," *Journal of African American History* 91, no. 2 (2006): 176.

47. Clayborne Carson, *Malcolm X: The FBI File* (New York: Carroll & Graf, 1991), 48, 49.

48. Jonathan Bradley, "Churchville, John, 1941–," *The Online Reference Guide to African American History*, accessed October 30, 2018,

https://blackpast.org/aah/churchville-john-1941; Churchville, email message to author, October 12, 2018.

49. John Elliot Churchville, "Dear Mr. Churchville: July 30, 1965"
(New York: Schomburg Center for Research in Black Culture, July 30,
1965), 1.

50. Annmarie Bean, "The Free Southern Theater: Mythology and Mov-
ing Between Movements," in *Restaging the Sixties: Radical Theaters and
Their Legacies,* ed. James M. Harding and Cindy Rosenthal (Ann Arbor:
University of Michigan Press, 2006), 263; "Visual and Performing Arts in
Libraries," *An Interpretation of the Library Bill of Rights,* American Library
Association, accessed November 3, 2018, www.ala.org/advocacy/intfree
dom/librarybill/interpretations/arts.

51. Todd London, *An Ideal Theater: Founding Visions for a New
American Art* (New York: Theater Communications Group, 2013), 121;
Genevieve Fabre, *Drumbeats, Masks and Metaphor: Contemporary Afro-
American Theatre* (Cambridge: Harvard University Press, 1983), 18.

52. John O'Neal, "A General Prospectus for the Establishment of a
Free Southern Theater," in *The Free Southern Theater, by the Free South-
ern Theater: A Documentary of the South's Radical Black Theater, with Jour-
nals, Letters, Poetry, Essays, and a Play Written by Those Who Built It,* ed.
Thomas C. Dent, Richard Schechner, and Gilbert Moses (Indianapolis:
Bobbs-Merrill, 1969), 27–28.

53. Ibid., 179.

54. Ibid.; "Visual and Performing Arts in Libraries."

55. Denise Nicholas, "Preliminary Proposal for An Afro*American/
African Information Center" (New York: Schomburg Center for Research
in Black Culture, n.d.), 5; "The Ghetto of Desire" heading is taken from
one of the FST's plays: *The Desire.*

56. O'Neal, "A General Prospectus for the Establishment of a Free
Southern Theater," 181–85.

57. Ibid.; Lewis Michaux was a long-time Black nationalist and had
operated his bookstore in Harlem since 1932. Boasting the largest stock
anywhere of books by and about African Americans, the store was also a
reading library for many who could simply not afford to purchase a book.
Ghana's first president shopped there, and so did Malcolm X and Langston
Hughes. W. E. B. Du Bois met his wife there while browsing the shelves.

58. Denise Nicholas, "View from The Free Southern Theater," *Liberator* (New York) 6 (1966).

59. Genevieve Fabre, *Drumbeats, Masks and Metaphor: Contemporary
Afro-American Theatre* (Cambridge: Harvard University Press, 1983), 18;

O'Neal, "A General Prospectus for the Establishment of a Free Southern Theater," 229; Kent B. Germany, *New Orleans after the Promises: Poverty, Citizenship, and the Search for the Great Society* (Athens: University of Georgia Press, 2007), 70; The Desire housing project is the same place Tennessee Williams used for *A Streetcar Named Desire*.

60. O'Neal, "A General Prospectus for the Establishment of a Free Southern Theater," 184.

61. Denise Nicholas, *Freshwater Road* (Evanston, IL: Agate, 2005), 312.

CHAPTER SEVEN

1. Sanderia Faye, *Mourner's Bench* (Fayetteville: University of Arkansas Press, 2015), 325.

2. Randy Finley, "Crossing the White Line: SNCC in Three Delta Towns, 1963–1967," in *Arsnick: The Student Nonviolent Coordinating Committee in Arkansas*, ed. Jennifer Jensen Wallach and John A. Kirk (Fayetteville: University of Arkansas Press, 2011), 66.

3. Laura Foner, "Arkansas SNCC Memories," in *Arsnick: The Student Nonviolent Coordinating Committee in Arkansas*, ed. Jennifer Jensen Wallach and John A. Kirk (Fayetteville: University of Arkansas Press, 2011), 105.

4. Brent Riffel, "In the Storm: William Hansen and the Student Nonviolent Coordinating Committee in Arkansas, 1962–1967," in *Arsnick: The Student Nonviolent Coordinating Committee in Arkansas*, ed. Jennifer Jensen Wallach and John A. Kirk (Fayetteville: University of Arkansas Press, 2011), 29.

5. Jacob Rosenberg, "Elaine's History Resurfaces in a Documentary 100 Years Later," *Arkansas Times* (Little Rock), November 16, 2017.

6. Melba Pattillo Beals, *Warriors Don't Cry: A Searing Memoir of the Battle to Integrate Little Rock's Central High* (New York: Pocket Books, 1994), 23–24.

7. Ibid., 171; Melba Pattillo Beals, email message to author, January 14, 2019.

8. John A. Kirk, "Facilitating Change: The Arkansas Council on Human Relations, 1954–1964," accessed December 12, 2018, http://plaza.ufl.edu/wardb/Kirk.doc.

9. Dorothy Miller, "To Nat Griswold," University of Arkansas Special Collections, Little Rock, series 1, box 33, folder 335.

10. Cheryl Knott, *Not Free, Not for All: Public Libraries in the Age of Jim Crow* (Boston: University of Massachusetts Press, 2015), 7.

11. Ibid., 257.

12. Terence Roberts, email message to author, January 12, 2019.

13. Ibid.

14. Gertrude Newsom Jackson, "Oral History Interview," *Library of Congress* video, November 11, 2010, www.loc.gov/item/afc2010039_crhp0004.

15. Ibid.

16. Beals, email message to author, January 14, 2019.

17. Riffel, "In the Storm," 26; David Smith, "Little Rock Nine: The Day Young Students Shattered Racial Segregation," *The Guardian* (London), September 24, 2017, www.theguardian.com/world/2017/sep/24/little-rock-arkansas-school-segregation-racism; William Hansen, email message to author, January 2, 2019. While his ribs healed, Hansen's teeth were—and continue to be—problematic for him.

18. Riffel, "In the Storm," 27.

19. Riffel, "In the Storm," 27.

20. Finley, "Crossing the White Line," 58.

21. Hansen, email message to author, January 2, 2019.

22. Ibid.

23. Grif Stockley, *Ruled by Race: Black/White Relations in Arkansas from Slavery to the Present* (Fayetteville: University of Arkansas Press, 2009), 333.

24. Riffel, "In the Storm," 64; "What Is the Summer Project," State Historical Society of Wisconsin, Madison, 1965, p. 2.

25. Hansen, email message to author, January 2, 2019; Riffel, "In the Storm," 64.

26. Foner, "Arkansas SNCC Memories," 150.

27. Riffel, "In the Storm," 64; Foner, "Arkansas SNCC Memories," 151; Stockley, *Ruled by Race*, 343.

28. Laura Foner, interview with author, February 5, 2018.

29. Ibid.

30. Ibid.

31. Ibid.

32. Riffel, "In the Storm," 65.

33. Foner, "Arkansas SNCC Memories," 150.

34. Laura Foner, "Civil Rights Actions in Arkansas," C-SPAN video, July 9, 2011, www.c-span.org/video/?300407-2/civil-rights-actions-arkansas.

35. Foner, "Arkansas SNCC Memories," 151.

36. Foner, "Civil Rights Actions in Arkansas."

37. Foner, "Arkansas SNCC Memories," 152.

38. Laura Foner, email message to author, January 15, 2019.

39. Finley, "Crossing the White Line," 66.

40. Brenda Everett, "The Freedom School Library," *Gould Freedom News*, 1965, 1 (author's possession).

41. Ibid.

42. Myrtle Glascoe, "Oral History Interview," *Library of Congress* video, November 11, 2010, www.loc.gov/item/2015669102.

43. Finley, "Crossing the White Line," 67.

44. Jennifer Jensen Wallach, "An Interview with Millard 'Tex' Lowe," in *Arsnick: The Student Nonviolent Coordinating Committee in Arkansas*, ed. Jennifer Jensen Wallach and John A. Kirk (Fayetteville: University of Arkansas Press, 2011), 146.

45. Millard Lowe, "Civil Rights Actions in Arkansas," C-SPAN video, July 9, 2011, www.c-span.org/video/?300407-2/civil-rights-actions-arkansas.

46. Millard Lowe, email message to author, January 21, 2019.

47. Lowe, "Civil Rights Actions in Arkansas."

48. Lowe, email message to author, January 21, 2019.

49. Michael Simmons, "Arkansas Roots and Consciousness," in *Arsnick: The Student Nonviolent Coordinating Committee in Arkansas*, ed. Jennifer Jensen Wallach and John A. Kirk (Fayetteville: University of Arkansas Press, 2011), 112.

50. Riffel, "In the Storm," 33.

51. Peniel E. Joseph, *Stokely: A Life* (New York: Civitas Books, 2014), 115.

52. Foner, "Arkansas SNCC Memories," 154; Foner, interview with author, February 5, 2018.

53. Foner, interview with author, February 5, 2018.

54. Rebeca Oliveira, "Connolly Children's Librarian to Retire," *Jamaica Plain Gazette* (Jamaica Plain, MA), June 26, 2014, http://jamaicaplaingazette.com/2014/06/06/connolly-childrens-librarian-to-retire.

55. Foner, interview with author, February 5, 2018.

56. Ibid.

57. Ibid.

Chapter Eight

1. Peter Abrahams, *Tell Freedom: Memories of Africa* (New York: Alfred A. Knopf, 1954), 224–26; Maxine K. Rochester, "The Carnegie Corporation and South Africa; Non-European Library Services," *Libraries & Culture* 34, no. 1 (1999): 28–51. The Bantu Men's Social Centre's collection was part of library services provided to Black South Africans—the "Non-Europeans"—by the Carnegie Corporation of New York during the 1920s and 1930s. While it may seem odd to provide the titles mentioned in the collection to a target audience that not only had limited experience with books and reading but also knew English only as a second language, these titles were the most popular and requested ones. As librarian for the Carnegie Library Service for Non-Europeans, playwright Herbert Dhlomo helped select these titles, knowing from his own work that books by African Americans helped inspire and encourage Black Africans. The Centre itself was absorbed into the Johannesburg Public Library in 1940 as one of its segregated branches. Segregated library service remained in South Africa until 1990.

2. Jonathan L. Walton, "Afterword: Dignity as a Weapon of Love," in *To Shape a New World: Essays on the Political Philosophy of Martin Luther King, Jr.*, ed. Tommie Shelby and Brandon M. Terry (Cambridge: Belknap Press of Harvard University Press, 2018), 348. The exact quote is "dignity is an orientation that ought to recognize itself in others." The author has paraphrased it, but full credit is Walton's.

3. "The Civil Rights Movement: Why Now?" *Tolerance.org*, last modified March 2014, www.tolerance.org/magazine/publications/teaching-the-movement-2014/the-civil-rights-movement-why-now; J. Todd Moye, *Ella Baker: Community Organizer of the Civil Rights Movement* (Lanham, MD: Rowman & Littlefield, 2013), 1; Casper L. Jordan, "Library Service to Black Americans," *Library Trends* 20 (1971): 273.

4. Stephen Cresswell, "The Last Days of Jim Crow in Southern Libraries," *Libraries & Culture* 31, no. 3 (1996): 567; Donald G. Davis Jr. and Cheryl Knott Malone, "Reading for Liberation: The Role of Libraries in the 1964 Mississippi Freedom Summer Project," in *Untold Stories: Civil Rights, Libraries, and Black Librarianship*, ed. John Mark Tucker (Champaign: Graduate School of Library and Information Sciences, University of Illinois, 1998), pp. 120, 122; Susan Lee Scott, "Integration of Public Libraries in the South: Attitudes and Actions of the Library Profession," *Southeastern Librarian* (Fall 1968): 168.

5. G. Edward Evans and Margaret Zarnosky Saponaro, *Collection Management Basics* (Santa Barbara, CA: Libraries Unlimited, 2012), 39.

6. Sally Belfrage, *Freedom Summer* (Charlottesville: University of Virginia Press, 1999), 47.

7. Carol Smallwood, ed., *The Frugal Librarian: Thriving in Tough Economic Times* (Chicago: American Library Association, 2011). Cover copy.

8. Charlie Bennett, "The Library Is Not a Collection of Books," filmed March 1, 2014, in Augusta, TEDx video, 11:15, www.youtube.com/watch?v=tFGCB51xb6U.

9. Danielle Allen, "Integration, Freedom, and the Affirmation of Life," in *To Shape a New World: Essays on the Political Philosophy of Martin Luther King, Jr.*, ed. Tommie Shelby and Brandon M. Terry (Cambridge: Belknap Press of Harvard University Press, 2018), 155; Nancy C. Kranich, "Introduction," in *Libraries & Democracy: The Cornerstones of Liberty*, ed. Nancy C. Kranich (Chicago: American Library Association, 2001), 12.

10. Peniel E. Joseph, "Rethinking the Black Power Era," *Journal of Southern History* 75 (2009): 708.

11. Susan B. Kretchmer, "The First Amendment, Libraries, and Democracy," in *Libraries & Democracy: The Cornerstones of Liberty*, ed. Nancy C. Kranich (Chicago: American Library Association, 2001), 148; Karen Cook, *Freedom Libraries in the 1964 Mississippi Freedom Summer Project: A History* (Tuscaloosa: University of Alabama Press, 2008), xviii.

12. Charles Alexander Preston, "Feds Watching," *Facebook*, February 6, 2019, www.facebook.com/photo.php?fbid=10156733320751539&set=pcb.10156733321201539&type=3&theater.

Selected Bibliography

Battles, David M. *The History of Public Library Access for African Americans in the South, or, Leaving Behind the Plow*. Lanham, MD: Scarecrow Press, 2009.

Beals, Melba Pattillo. *Warriors Don't Cry: A Searing Memoir of the Battle to Integrate Little Rock's Central High*. New York: Pocket Books, 1994.

Belfrage, Sally. *Freedom Summer*. Charlottesville: University of Virginia Press, 1999.

Branch, Taylor. *At Canaan's Edge: America in the King Years, 1965–68*. New York: Simon & Schuster, 2007.

———. *Parting the Waters: America in the King Years, 1954–1963*. New York: Simon & Schuster Paperbacks, 1988.

———. *Pillar of Fire: America in the King Years, 1963–65*. New York: Simon & Schuster, 1998.

Cook, Karen. *Freedom Libraries in the 1964 Mississippi Freedom Summer Project: A History*. Tuscaloosa: University of Alabama Press, 2008.

Countryman, Matthew J. *Up South: Civil Rights and Black Power in Philadelphia*. Philadelphia: University of Pennsylvania Press, 2003.

Dent, Thomas C., Richard Schechner, Gilbert Moses, and the Free Southern Theater, eds. *The Free Southern Theater, by the Free Southern Theater: A Documentary of the South's Radical Black Theater, with Journals, Letters, Poetry, Essays, and a Play Written by Those Who Built It*. Indianapolis: Bobbs-Merrill, 1969.

Dittmer, John, *Local People: The Struggle for Civil Rights in Mississippi*. Champaign: University of Illinois Press, 1994.

Eagles, Charles W. *Outside Agitator: Jon Daniels and the Civil Rights Movement in Alabama*. Tuscaloosa: University of Alabama Press, 2000.

Early, Gerald L. *This Is Where I Came In: Black America in the 60s*. Lincoln: University of Nebraska, 2003.

Fabre, Genevieve. *Drumbeats, Masks and Metaphor: Contemporary Afro-American Theatre*. Cambridge: Harvard University Press, 1983.

Faye, Sanderia. *Mourner's Bench*. Fayetteville: University of Arkansas Press, 2015.

Gaillard, Frye. *Cradle of Freedom: Alabama and the Movement That Changed America*. Tuscaloosa: University of Alabama Press, 2004.

Graham, Patterson Toby. *The Right to Read: Segregation and Civil Rights in Alabama's Public Libraries*. Tuscaloosa: University of Alabama Press, 2002.

Halberstam, David. *The Children*. New York: Fawcett Press, 1999.

Hale, Jon N., and William Sturkey, eds. *To Write in the Light of Freedom: The Newspapers of the 1964 Mississippi Freedom Schools*. Jackson: University of Mississippi Press, 2015.

Holsaert, Faith S., ed. *Hands on the Freedom Plow: Personal Accounts by Women in SNCC*. Chicago: University of Illinois Press, 2012.

Huie, William Bradford. *Three Lives for Mississippi*. New York: Whitney Communications, 1965.

Jeffries, Hasan Kwame. *Bloody Lowndes: Civil Rights and Black Power in Alabama's Black Belt*. New York: New York University Press, 2009.

Joseph, Peniel E. *Stokely: A Life*. New York: Basic Civitas, 2014.

Katagiri, Yasuhiro. *The Mississippi State Sovereignty Commission: Civil Rights and States' Rights*. Jackson: University Press of Mississippi, 2001.

King, Martin Luther, Jr. *The Autobiography of Martin Luther King Jr*. Edited by Clayborne Carson. New York: Warner Books, 2001.

Knott, Cheryl. *Not Free, Not for All: Public Libraries in the Age of Jim Crow*. Boston: University of Massachusetts Press, 2015.

Kranich, Nancy C., ed. *Libraries & Democracy: The Cornerstones of Liberty*. Chicago: American Library Association, 2001.

Leventhal, Willy S. *The Scope of Freedom: The Leadership of Hosea Williams with Dr. King's Summer '65 Student Volunteers*. Montgomery, AL: Challenge Publishing, 2005.

McMillen, Neil R. *The Citizens' Council: Organized Resistance to the Second Reconstruction*. Urbana: University of Illinois Press, 1994.

Mendelsohn, Jack. *The Martyrs: Sixteen Who Gave Their Lives for Racial Justice*. New York: Harper and Row, 1966.

Nicholas, Denise. *Freshwater Road*. Evanston, IL: Agate, 2005.

O'Reilly, Kenneth. *Racial Matters: The FBI's Secret File on Black America, 1960–1972*. New York: Free Press, 1991.

Sojourner, Sue, and Cheryl Reitan. *Thunder of Freedom: Black Leadership and the Transformation of 1960s Mississippi*. Lexington: University of Kentucky Press, 2013.

Stockley, Grif. *Ruled by Race: Black/White Relations in Arkansas from Slavery to the Present*. Fayetteville: University of Arkansas Press, 2009.

Tucker, John Mark, ed. *Untold Stories: Civil Rights, Libraries, and Black Librarianship*. Champaign: Graduate School of Library and Information Sciences, University of Illinois, 1998.

Wallach, Jennifer Jensen, and John A. Kirk, eds. *Arsnick: The Student Nonviolent Coordinating Committee in Arkansas*. Fayetteville: University of Arkansas Press, 2011.

Watson, Bruce. *Freedom Summer: The Savage Summer That Made Mississippi Burn and Made America a Democracy*. New York: Penguin Books, 2010.

Wiegand, Wayne A. *Part of Our Lives: A People's History of the American Public Library*. New York: Oxford University Press, 2016.

Zitter, Sarai G. *Memoirs of a Fortunate Life: The Evolution of an Activist*. Baltimore: PublishAmerica, 2011.

Index

About the Author

Mike Selby is an information professional, a public librarian, and a popular newspaper columnist. He has published over one thousand articles on print culture, libraries, and the Civil Rights Movement. His work has also been featured in peer-reviewed journals and the Library History Roundtable of the American Library Association. He received his MLIS from the University of Alabama, and lives and practices librarianship in the Rocky Mountains of British Columbia.

His work on librarians during the Civil Rights Movement has been featured in the peer-reviewed journal *Feliciter*, and his discovery of two Freedom Libraries in Alabama was also published in the journal *The Southeastern Librarian*. He has written extensively on the grim history of library segregation in his newspaper column, "Mike's Booknotes." He has been the information services librarian for the Cranbrook Public Library for more than a dozen years. His history of that library was published with acclaim on *ALA Library History Roundtable News & Notes* blog.

During his graduate work at the University of Alabama, he first learned about the Freedom Libraries in Mississippi, which had only come to light in 2008. Although he was told point blank that none had existed in Alabama, this turned out not to be true at all. His research uncovered two in that state. The courage and violence and legacy of these two had to be told, and his findings were published in the journal *The Southeastern Librarian*.